Awaken the Stars

Awaken the Stars

reflections on what we REALLY teach

Essays by 25 Distinguished Professors at the University of Portland
Edited by Shannon Mayer and Jacquie Van Hoomissen

AWAKEN THE STARS
Reflections on What We *Really* Teach
Edited by Shannon Mayer and Jacquie Van Hoomissen

Design and typesetting by Patricia A. Lynch
Cover art under license from Bigstock

Published by ACTA Publications, 4848 N. Clark St., Chicago, IL 60640
800-397-2282, www.actapublications.com

Scripture quotations are from the *New Revised Standard Version Bible*, copyright © 1989 by the Division of Christian Education of the National Council of the Churches of Christ in the USA. Used by permission.

Library of Congress Catalog number: 2017931247
ISBN: 978-0-87946-587-2
Printed in the United States of America by Total Printing Systems
Year 30 29 28 27 26 25 24 23 22 21 20 19 18 17
Printing 15 14 13 12 11 10 9 8 7 6 5 4 3 2 First

♻ Text printed on 30% post-consumer waste paper

CONTENTS

PART III. THRIVE

PART IV. ENGAGE

Dedication

With gratitude to Brian Doyle
Editor of *Portland Magazine*
University of Portland

You taught us all how to
Awaken the Stars.

A note from the editors

Shannon Mayer
Department of Physics
University of Portland

Jacquie Van Hoomissen
Department of Biology
University of Portland

We asked some of our fellow faculty members at the University of Portland, a Holy Cross institution in the Pacific Northwest, what it is they *really* teach. This essay collection, by twenty-five professors of various academic disciplines at the university, was written in response to this question.

We hope the book will be an invitation to look beyond what is in the course catalog, class syllabi, or reading list at any college or university and to encounter the richer and deeper and more meaningful story of what happens (or should happen) in the classrooms and professors' offices and libraries and field trips and internships and study-abroad programs in the United States and around the globe.

For the educator, perhaps this collection will prompt you to reflect on what it is that you really teach. Consideration of that question will encourage you to be attentive and awake in a fresh way as you engage students.

For students, parents, alumni, and others interested in a deeper look at the world of academia, we designed this book to surprise and inspire you. We trust, of course, that the essays will be thought provoking and enjoyable to read, and that some story or anecdote will settle in you in a lasting and meaningful way. But beyond that, we hope the essays will provide you with an inspiring picture of what higher education really should be all about.

INTRODUCTION

Father Mark Poorman, CSC
President, University of Portland

"Wherever we work we assist others not only to recognize and develop their own gifts but also to discover the deepest longing in their lives. And, as in every work of our mission, we find that we ourselves stand to learn much from those whom we are called to teach."
—Congregation of Holy Cross Constitutions, Constitution II

It is not an overstatement to say that higher education is undergoing a shift of massive proportions. More and more, we are called upon to explain ourselves, to offer the employment statistics of our graduates as justification of cost, to focus our resources in areas with direct links to lucrative careers, to make clear the monetary value of our courses and degrees and certificates we offer prospective students. And while "return on investment" is an uncomfortable phrase for many of us in education, it also offers us an important opportunity to turn inward, to take stock, and to make sure that who we are is reflected in what we *really* teach. Indeed, I would argue that the term includes much more than our seniors' job prospects and starting salaries. As the Holy Cross Constitutions quoted above suggest, it includes the outcome of our efforts to help our students "discover the deepest longing in their lives." It is a tall order, to be sure, and one that takes great courage and commitment to aspire to and achieve.

Awaken the Stars is an invitation into the world of the talented and accomplished faculty members at the University of Portland, who have made it their life's work to guide students on that road to self-discovery. They bring a different voice to the conversation about the value of higher education—speaking of wonder, empathy, growth, and discomfort. The content of their courses is not unimportant, but rather it is informed and enriched by these greater goods that push our students to be the persons they are called to be. These faculty members are truly *teachers* in the fullest sense of the word.

Teaching is one of the greatest sources of joy among my vocational commitments, and one I was unwilling to give up when I became president. That is why each spring I co-teach an upper-level Theology course called "The Character Project" with three colleagues. Every week, we challenge the juniors and seniors in the course to give voice to the deepest parts of themselves, to reconcile the people they believe themselves to be with the decisions they make and actions they take each and every day. After several years of teaching the course, it has become apparent to me that the students who benefit most are those who struggle to create and articulate a moral frame on which they can hang their lives. The responsibility for us as teachers is to help our students understand that they must be active participants in the creation of their own character and to insist they do so even in the face of discomfort or adversity. As this collection of essays illustrates, this responsibility is not relegated to any single discipline but is present in everything from quantum mechanics to anatomy to liberal arts to my Monday evening theology course.

It is my strong belief that this approach to education—engaging and guiding our students' minds and hearts—is becoming increasingly rare, and therefore increasingly valuable. It remains a hallmark of a University of Portland education and of the Congregation of Holy Cross, the religious order of priests and brothers that

> The responsibility for us as teachers is to help our students understand that they must be active participants in the creation of their own character and to insist they do so even in the face of discomfort or adversity.

founded the University of Portland and several other colleges and universities across the country. In Holy Cross, we are called to be educators in the faith and, in the oft-repeated words of our founder, Blessed Basil Moreau, believe strongly that "the mind will not be cultivated at the expense of the heart." At the University of Portland, our faculty members renew and live out that commitment every day, encouraging our students to go beyond their comfort zones, beyond the knowledge required to ace the test or pass the class, to see the *real* learning that lies beneath.

As the essays in this collection show, our students, on both the undergraduate and graduate levels, are taught to challenge their assumptions about the universe and to see how what they choose to pay attention to helps define the world around them. They encounter professors who genuinely believe that who students are as individuals is far more important than what external triumph or failure they are currently living through. These professors teach them to embrace discomfort as a sign of personal growth and to cultivate a creative engagement with their studies as an opportunity for self-discovery.

I am humbled and honored to work alongside such talented faculty colleagues every day. Each essay in this book confirms for me the value of a Holy Cross education and inspires me to continue seeking opportunities to unsettle my students in the hope they will learn much more than the syllabi suggest. I hope that you, too, come away from this book with a greater appreciation of all that higher education can offer when we demand that it not only teach students how to transform the world but also how, with the grace of God, to transform themselves.

Part I

Awaken

"Wonder is the beginning of wisdom."—Greek Proverb

Prologue

Jacquie Van Hoomissen

*E*veryone has a story about that one moment when things changed and the world was different. Maybe this turning point altered the trajectory of a life or opened new eyes to the beauty of the universe, and the impact was meaningful enough to be remembered. The more we recall these moments, the more powerful they become in the life narrative we each write and expand upon with every new educational experience. The teachers in the following section all speak of moments when the minds of their students are awakened to wonder, to revelation, to perspectives that spark new insights into understanding the mystery of the world.

Professor of Wonder

Shannon Mayer

Physics Professor Shannon Mayer specializes in optics, with particular interest in the fields of quantum optics, laser spectroscopy, physics education, and science policy. She has published her work in technical journals, teaching journals, conference proceedings, and book chapters.

*W*onder as a verb is an action, an impulse: *to think or speculate curiously; to be filled with admiration, amazement, or awe; to marvel.* Like gravity, the question "I wonder?" is a force of nature. It is the force that has propelled scientists, theologians, and explorers alike on the unstoppable quest to discover the story of our world. It is inborn and intrinsic, an inherent part of the fabric of human nature—as watching any small child learn will prove. But, again like gravity, which diminishes as you get further from the source of the gravitational pull, the force of wonder tends to diminish the further one gets from childhood. Other forces (fear, indolence, busyness, the prescriptiveness of formal education, etc.) conspire against wonder to weaken its power.

Consider wonder the noun: *a feeling of surprise mingled with admiration, caused by something beautiful, unexpected, unfamiliar, or inexplicable.* Wonder sneaks up on us in ways we aren't expecting. An encounter with unexpected beauty, a glimpse of the astonishing cleverness of nature, serves to deepen our friendship with wonder. Like its cousin, joy, wonder is a signpost that hints of a deeper, more profound mystery in the story of our world.

Me, I was drawn to physics by a love of mathematics. As I often tell my students, mathematics is the language of science and to do science you need to learn to speak the language. For those who do speak the language, mathematics can be a purveyor of wonder; it possesses an artistic beauty akin to a beautiful painting or an intricate and melodic symphony. The fact that the universe is, at some level, describable by humans using beautiful mathematical equations is truly remarkable. Paul Dirac, a brilliant pioneer of quantum mechanics, believed that beauty was an essential feature of mathematical equations suited to the description of the physical world. Einstein once said that the most incomprehensible thing about the universe is that it is comprehensible. How do we happen to live in a universe we can describe using the language of mathematics? Why do humans have the desire and, more remarkably, the capacity to understand the mathematics that describes the world? These are all questions that bring me back to wonder.

Artists often have a favorite painting or sculpture that has become an intimate companion on their journey of wonder. For a musician, it may be a particular symphony that inspires awe. For me, a physicist, the masterpiece I most admire is a particularly *beautiful* equation. Its formal name is The Wave Equation and in the language of mathematic it looks like this:

$$\nabla^2 \psi = \frac{1}{v^2} \frac{\partial^2 \psi}{\partial t^2}$$

A mathematician would call this a second-order, linear, partial-differential equation, but don't let the formidable title scare you away. Let me introduce you to a few of the beautiful features of this equation.

The wave equation is simultaneously elegant in its simplicity and profound in its versatility. It was first studied in the 1700s by Jean-Baptiste le Rond d'Alembert, who derived the equation to describe the vibration of a musical string. Since that humble beginning, the wave equation has been found to be equally at home in the cultured world of the concert music hall, among the bravado and swagger of big wave surfers in Hawaii, and out in the cold and empty space of space. Anywhere we encounter a wave, be it mechanical (a vibrating guitar string), acoustic (the campus bell tower chiming), or electromagnetic (sunshine streaming in your window this morning), the wave equation is there. The fact that so many seemingly different phenomena can be accurately described by the same mathematical equation is, to me, part of its beauty.

In addition to its versatility, the wave equation has great intuition, so to speak; it has the insight to predict that when two waves interact with one another, they superimpose, or add together. This is consistent with our experience with waves. When we drop two pebbles into smooth water simultaneously and watch the ripples travel outward, meet each other, dance together for a moment, and then continue unperturbed on their individual ways, they are fulfilling the requirements of the wave equation. In contrast, particles, when they interact, scatter off one another like billiard balls, permanently altering the path of the other by their interaction.

The predictive ability of the wave equation is another of its impressive facets. In the mid-1800s, the physicist James Clerk Maxwell was puttering around with the mathematical equations known at the time to describe electrical and magnetic phenomena: circuits, magnets, and the like. What he found, if he combined these equations in *just* the right way, is that they *predicted* that electric and magnetic fields *themselves* could be described as waves. The wave equation applied to them too. The mathematics is the same, the application completely different. When Maxwell used his newly derived wave equation and computed the speed of these predicted traveling electric and magnetic waves, he discovered that they moved along at a speed eerily close to the accepted value of the speed of light. The remarkable beauty of his mathematics thus compelled him to propose that light itself was a form of traveling electric and magnetic fields. Maxwell's proposal, and the simple, beautiful mathematics behind it, turned the world of physics upside down. The notion that light itself was a traveling electromagnetic wave was revolutionary; it brought together the seemingly separate disciplines of electricity, magnetism, and optics, and foreshadowed some of the weird and wonderful aspects of the world of quantum mechanics.

Wonder, I think, captures the essence of *everything* that we are about in higher education and anywhere real teaching is taking place. My craft, as a physicist, is to

> *Wonder*, I think, captures the essence of *everything* that we are about in higher education and anywhere real teaching is taking place.

pursue wonder. My charge, as a professor of physics, is to empower students to become wonderers and, in the process of wondering itself, to make discoveries about our remarkable and curious world. My colleagues in the other disciplines likewise profess wonder in endless forms. Scientist or philosopher, theologian or poet, we all seek to use the tools of our particular trade to probe the mysteries of the universe. Encountering the universe with wonder is our common enterprise. Indeed we are all professors of wonder, at a University of Wonder, and that is, well, wonderful.

Touched by the Infinite

Rev. Charles McCoy, CSC

Mathematics Professor and Holy Cross priest Fr. Charles McCoy, CSC, studies a branch of mathematical logic that analyzes the relative complexity of constructions and theorems in other areas of mathematics, such as modern algebra and analysis. He has collaborated with mathematicians from a variety of countries, and his research teams have published their work in U.S. and Russian journals. A National Science Foundation grant specifically dedicated to international collaboration has supported these endeavors.

When people first learn that I am a Holy Cross priest and a college professor, they often ask, "Do you teach theology?" When I respond that I teach mathematics, some respond with a puzzled look that implicitly asks, "How do those two parts of your life go together?" (Or, more rarely, the bold will say the question out loud.) Throughout my own journey in academia and in religious life, I've meditated on this question for myself, and over the years I've realized that what intrigues me about mathematics is similar to what has called me to a life dedicated to my faith. Both entail the mystifying, fascinating, sometimes frustrating, always humbling contemplation of the Infinite.

The first college-level mathematics course that exposes students to the depth and mystery of the infinite is second-semester Calculus. The notion of "limit" (the idea of approximating function outputs to any given precision by approximating function inputs to a corresponding precision), encountered earlier in a student's mathematical journey, is certainly a difficult and subtle concept, and clarifying this concept in the eighteenth and nineteenth centuries was an enormous intellectual achievement for humanity. Nevertheless, the take-away of this idea, when applied to limits at infinity, is that if the limit exists then you can approximate that limit to any given precision by looking at a big enough finite input. (Of course, in application, the difficulty is ascertaining how big is "big enough.") This may leave novice mathematics students with the false (but philosophically easier to grasp) impression that "I can know infinity by extrapolating what I know about really big things."

In second-semester Calculus, however, students explore a concept that disturbs this naïve comfort with the infinite. The spoiler is infinite series. A series is a sum of infinitely many terms that can still add up to a finite number; an easy example is how $\frac{1}{3} = 0.3 + 0.03 + 0.003 + \ldots$. Now, at first it would seem that the insights into infinity gained by looking at series shouldn't be any different from the insights from Calculus I, for indeed series are technically defined with the same Calculus I concept of limit. However, when students try to apply their long familiarity with finite sums—after all they likely have been adding numbers since pre-school!—to the infinite counterpart, they discover that, in some ways, the behavior of infinite series simply has no analogue among finite sums. For instance, start with any sum S containing a finite number of terms, i.e., $S = a_1 + a_2 + a_3 + \ldots$. Re-arrange the order of the terms to your heart's content, and add them up in this new order; the Commutative Law of Addition guarantees that you will always get the same sum S. But the same is not always true for infinite series. For if we start with the infinite series: $1 - \frac{1}{2} + \frac{1}{3} - \frac{1}{4} + \frac{1}{5} - \frac{1}{6} + \ldots$, *the exact same set of terms* can be rearranged to give a sum of whatever positive or negative number one pleases! This complete breakdown in the "obvious" Commutative Law of Addition shakes our naïve confidence in the analogy between the infinite and the "really big finite."

There is a very important counterpart in religious awareness. People of faith, myself included, often intuitively or even explicitly think about God as an infinite analogue of ourselves. God is Father, so the divine must be a perfect version of my father; God is Love, so the divine must embody a kind of perfection, a limit, of human love. Under this paradigm, I understand God by extrapolating from what I know about the human person and human experience. But both the Hebrew and Christian Scriptures and the great Christian theologians and mystics warn us of the limitations or pitfalls in this line of thinking. As is the case with infinite series, sometimes the analogies dramatically break down; sometimes the truth about God is best understood in how God is not like us, instead of how God is the "infinite limit" of us. This is a deep truth underneath the terse claims that "God's ways are not our ways," or that God is "holy," whose meaning, we often forget, is: "other, different, set apart."

And yet, neither in the study of mathematics nor in the life of faith is this "otherness" a cause to abandon hope for knowledge or understanding. On the contrary, in the twentieth century, a new appreciation of infinity and its special intricacies opened up entirely new fields of mathematics and, perhaps more importantly, set all of mathematics on a new foundation. Similarly, the mystery and transcendence of God do not preclude prayerful meditation and theological reasoning; instead they provide the necessary foundation for such faithful endeavors to be genuine paths to truth. Perhaps no Christian belief about God is as "other," as different from human composition, as doctrine of the Trinity: that God is both perfectly One and perfectly Three. Yet, over the course of two millennia, theologians have developed a rich and positive Trinitarian theology that has impacted not only Christians' intellectual understanding but also our spirituality and even our moral vision of community.

> When we encounter Otherness and Mystery, we do not turn away in utter confusion; instead, we are drawn in and are capable of understanding, albeit incompletely.

Finally, then, in both mathematics and faith I see beauty and wonder. The Infinite has truly touched us. We may mistakenly begin by imagining the Infinite as something familiar, simply a better version of ourselves. Yet, when disabused of this notion, when we encounter Otherness and Mystery, we do not turn away in utter confusion; instead, we are drawn in and are capable of understanding, albeit incompletely. And in this capacity for genuine communion with the Infinite, we discover what is most mysterious in ourselves.

From Human Anatomy to Humanness

Jacquie Van Hoomissen

Biology Professor Jacquie Van Hoomissen studies the beneficial effects of physical activity on brain function, mental health, and well-being. She has published her work in neuroscience and public health journals and the popular press, and she has received national and local grants to support her research as well as her science education and outreach efforts.

I am fascinated with life. Not the chronological marching of time that defines the beginning and end, but how we, as humans, exist and coexist within the totality of everything else, the intriguing, complex, and sometimes mystifying *stuff* that just *is*. You could say I am fascinated by our *humanness*, by our existence in comparison to all else. What does it mean to be uniquely human? I want to know how we define "humanness" and share that experience with students. Is it possible to complete the definition of what it means to be human by learning all there is to know about how we are put together? If we look deep enough beneath our skin will the answer be there, bounding around our cells and illuminating the inner darkness? I teach Human Anatomy because it is a place to develop our definition of humanness, a discipline in which we puzzle-piece our structures together to understand what it means to be *us*.

Humanness is both something to know structurally but also something that transcends structure. It is a mystery to discover deep within ourselves. Anatomy is a place to start, a place to figure out what we know about our own physical make-up. It helps form a map of how we are put together, but the map falls drastically short when we try to understand ourselves and what makes us uniquely human. For that we have to dig deeper and go beyond the standard anatomical classification system that simplifies and normalizes every human body into the same alpha-numeric code in an anatomical reference book. Within this text of tight typographical structures, of indentations and font changes, there *must* be a place for difference, for nuances of design, for uniqueness that is impossible to catego-rize. In essence, there must be room for *humanness*.

Through the exploration of a human cadaver, students write their own defini-tion of humanness by engaging in what it means to be us—to ask questions, to pon-der options, to explore our own existence. This experience is profoundly challenging. Students experience discomfort, frustra-tion, accomplishment, baby steps forward, backwards steps, long and short lists of terms, gross things—like cadaver fingernails with nail polish. But they also discov-er the camaraderie gained through a shared, transfor-mational adventure and a deepening sense of purpose. Anatomy lab provides the catalyst. The experience push-es students to see *themselves* differently and to under-stand that it is impossible to *really* know every structure

> I was once that student, the one asking the questions they now ask of me about our bodies and what it means to be human.

of the body, because our knowledge is incomplete. In other words, we are still unsure of what it fully means to be human.

From my side of the chalkboard, I understand the struggle my students go through in class trying to wrap their minds around understanding themselves from a structural perspective. I was once that stu-dent, the one asking the questions they now ask of me about our bodies and what it means to be human. I was the panicked student trying to figure out how I could possibly learn every structure on the ca-daver, making endless notecards for ref-erence, drawing pathways of blood flow in my free time, staying up late into the night in the ca-daver laboratory, finding classmates who were willing to study with me so I could teach them because I knew by doing this I would learn the material even better. It was darn hard, and I'm sure at some point I shed more than one tear. I persevered long enough, however, until one day the terms were easier to say, the structures no lon-ger seemed randomly organized, organ systems started to come together, and finally the human body began to make sense to me. All the words, the vast array of complex terms derived from languages I didn't speak, added up to a human body, but the body I was looking at on the dissection table wasn't just a teaching tool, it wasn't an "it," he or she was a person…a beautiful, intricate, amazing person who was a mirror to my own design.

How remarkable to be human. How fascinating to see how we are stitched together and in what ways each structure supports another, summing to something greater that we can fully comprehend. How extraordinary to be human and possess the capacity to persevere in the pursuit of knowledge about our own existence. Such self-awareness is unique in the animal kingdom.

I can't directly lead my students to the same insights I had as a student, but I can give them opportunities to write their own definitions within our classroom community. Throughout their study of anatomy students add to their vision and conceptions of their bodies while simultaneously learning more about themselves and their place in the world. These learning opportunities come in fits and starts when their initial conceptions confront reality. As we progress through the semester, students change. Their definition of humanness expands with each new insight. At first they start to recognize reality; cadavers look nothing like the perfect, multi-colored models and charts present in the anatomy lab. Then they start to identify inconsistencies; not all anatomical structures are identically created in different people. Finally, they question what we know; if we understand so much about the anatomy of the brain, why can't we detail where consciousness comes from? Their questions go deeper than wanting to know which blood vessel carries oxygenated blood to the toes. They start asking who came before our species, what structures are vital to life, what might be the next evolutionary adaptations, how do humans develop from a single cell to a newborn baby, how are we different from our animal relatives, why do some populations suffer from preventable diseases, why do specific anatomical structures take on such social and cultural relevance, why is their sister so ill, is cancer going to take their dad away from them? They ask questions spontaneously, in the quiet moments in lab, while we sit together in a community of learners at a small table covered in lower pelvic floor models or lumbar vertebrae or skull replicas of long-ago extinct hominid species.

I answer them the best I can, but always initially with a simple question, "What do you think?" Then I just listen as they pour out their inner thoughts about all things human. What students don't realize quite yet is that through the act of posing and pondering anatomical questions they write their own definition of *humanness*.

As a professor, I now teach the same class I once agonized over two decades ago. My students and I spend the semester figuring out how the body is puzzle-pieced together, structure to structure, but our experience goes beyond that. At some point in the semester our Human Anatomy class becomes a new one I call Humanness Studies. I hope my students recognize this transition. I trust they learn more than just names and structures. I want them to see how each of us is knitted together by an unfathomable number of structures we share with one another and with other species…and to understand how truly amazing that is. I want them to know that we're not just memorizing structures; we are really learning about being human. We are learning about ourselves, and this knowledge cannot be categorized, named, or pointed out on any anatomical chart or model. At the heart of it, I want them to see that *humanness* is unique and with this distinctiveness comes our capacity to persevere and change the world around us. Yet it all starts with understanding how the hip bone is connected to the thigh bone.

Not What You Thought

Maximilian Schlosshauer

Physics Professor Maximilian Schlosshauer is an expert in quantum theory and the foundations of quantum mechanics. He is the editor of the book *Elegance and Enigma: The Quantum Interviews* and author of the textbook *Decoherence and the Quantum-to-Classical Transition.*

As a child, I went through years of classical-piano instruction, memorizing piece after piece through hours of rote practice. Mostly, it was dreadful. Then, one day I went to a teacher who introduced me to the basics of jazz and blues, and he showed me how to use those basics for improvisation. I was instantly electrified. This was *exactly* the sound and the freedom I had been looking for. From that moment on, playing the piano turned into a joyful pastime fueled by undiminishing excitement.

Later, during high school, a similarly revelatory moment got me interested in physics. By happenstance, I had picked up a copy of a book on quantum mechanics by the physicist Werner Heisenberg, one of the great pioneers of quantum mechanics in the early twentieth century. In his book, Heisenberg traced the intellectual journey from the natural philosophy of the Pre-Socratics to modern quantum physics and showed how modern physics has upended our views of the workings of nature. Seeing the story and role of science portrayed in this way was unlike anything I had previously encountered. In this story, physics, rather than cementing the idea of a mechanistic clockwork universe, turned out to be challenging this very notion. What I gleaned from Heisenberg's writings intrigued me so much that eventually I decided to study physics and specialized in quantum mechanics because I wanted to rigorously understand what quantum mechanics is really telling us about the world.

Moments of excitement and revelation have informed my own life in such a profound way that I want my students to have similar experiences. As a teacher, I hope to prepare the intellectual ground on which students can develop their own feelings of awe about the world and about the role physics plays in unraveling the rules of the cosmic game. In light of this goal, physics becomes a means to an end—although a very effective means—for it reveals a much richer, more subtle, and immeasurably more surprising world than anyone would have imagined.

One idea that reverberates through modern physics is that actions matter: that we are not passive observers of nature but that our experiments give birth to phenomena that were not determined by anything that has gone before. That's the lesson of quantum mechanics. But the role of observation goes further, for relativity theory has done away with our most cherished assumptions of absolute time and space, replacing them with a fundamentally quirky world where moving clocks are found to run slow and moving objects are measured to be shorter than when they are at rest. The world is malleable to human actions and defined by our choice of what to observe in ways so fundamental no one could have foreseen them before the advent of modern physics. How could this realization, brought forth not by philosophical speculation but by the scientific enterprise itself, not be surprising and exciting?

For students to be confronted with these perplexing implications of physics makes for wonderful learning experiences. When students realize that the world isn't all what it seems to be, there is a sense of challenge to one's deepest intuitions, triggering feelings of surprise and curiosity. Such encounters help turn students into critical thinkers and humble citizens who throughout their lives have the capability to remain aware of the complexities inherent even in seemingly mundane matters.

But physics isn't exciting just because it often challenges our intuitions. Equally astonishing is the way

> **When students realize that the world isn't all what it seems to be, there is a sense of challenge to one's deepest intuitions, triggering feelings of surprise and curiosity.**

it makes comprehensible a vast array of phenomena through a small set of basic principles. In turn, these principles allow us to make predictions of awe-inspiring accuracy and scope, ranging from the farthest reaches of the universe to the mysterious workings of the atomic realm. When I explain to my students how we can know how hot our universe was a tiny fraction of a second after the Big Bang, or how we can weigh a single electron or count the number of particles in the observable universe, I see students' faces light up with the beginning realization that science, far from being scary and difficult, gives every one of us power.

Through these moments of excitement and discovery, students can reappraise their views of nature and transform how they see themselves and engage in the world. They feel enriched and more confident, knowing that through their study of physics they have tapped into something extraordinary and beautiful. And thus the ultimate aim of my teaching is to give genuine meaning to two well-worn stated goals: that the purpose of college is to open students' minds and to turn them into lifelong learners.

Faith, Hope, and Love: A Trinity of Uncertainty

Steven G. Mayer

Chemistry Professor Steven G. Mayer specializes in spectroscopy, with particular interest in the fields of nanoparticles, laser spectroscopy, experimental pedagogy, and undergraduate research. He has published his work in technical journals, teaching journals, conference proceedings, and book chapters.

The universe is beautiful and ordered and it appears to work in a manner that makes sense to us. Yet as we delve further into the structure of the universe at the extreme edges of small and large we find behavior that is surprising, outside the realm of what we would call "common sense." This behavior is intriguing and calls into question all we think we know. What if nature is, at a fundamental level, vastly different than we think? What If the surest thing in the universe is uncertainty?

My official title is Professor of Chemistry and my specialty is Physical Chemistry or, as I like to describe it, "the physics of chemistry." All physical objects are constructed of atoms—the building blocks of the natural world—so any physical phenomenon we observe must begin with atoms. We are inclined to think of atoms as well-defined physical objects, perhaps a little like very tiny marbles, because the macroscopic structures that are made of them are well-defined solid objects, such as salt crystals, or rocks, or humans. However, our best description of an atom is emphatically and unequivocally uncertain. Uncertainty isn't the same thing as ignorance or confusion. Uncertainty is a fundamental principle of physics and is written into the very fabric of the universe. Werner Heisenberg, one of the most famous physicists of all time, established that it is impossible to know exactly how fast a particle is traveling and its exact position at the same instant. This statement is now known as the Heisenberg Uncertainty Principle and is a standard topic in physics and chemistry curricula worldwide.

The simplest atom, hydrogen, is just a single proton and an electron. When the electron from one hydrogen atom occupies part of the space of another electron from another hydrogen atom, they become entangled; and this entanglement instantaneously results in the formation of a new chemical entity known as a hydrogen molecule. But here is the weird part; entanglement can only happen because the instantaneous positions and momenta of the electrons are not well-defined and therefore, the identities of the two electrons are uncertain. I don't mean philosophically uncertain, but physically uncertain—like two clones who not only look exactly alike but are so completely and utterly alike that even they can't tell themselves apart.

We base our understanding of atoms and molecules on the bedrock principle of uncertainty, but uncertainty also shows up in the Schrödinger equation, the mathematical relationship that we must solve in order to obtain a three-dimensional description of an atom or molecule. Consider this: Whatever shape a single atom or molecule takes dictates the shape and properties of the solid compound that you hold in your hand and observe with your eyes. So how is it that, in the presence of all this uncertainty, Michelangelo's David has been the same for hundreds of years and will likely remain so for hundreds more? The answer is that rather than talking about the positions or the momenta of the electrons, which we cannot know with arbitrary precision anyway, we instead talk about the probability of where the electrons can and cannot exist. If this probability is not changing in time, then the macroscopic properties of the material do not change in time either. Probability is perhaps a fuzzy concept as well, but it can be readily understood by considering the space swept out by a rotating three-blade fan. While the circular area defined by the radius of the fan blades is at any instant about half empty space, you still don't stick your finger into the area because the probability of injuring yourself is very high. Taking this analogy a bit further, the act of sticking your finger into the space where a blade could be allows you to observe the existence of the blade in that space. At the level of atoms, it is the act of observation that creates the existence of the physical entity. In other words, one's decision to observe something changes probability into reality!

So while atomic and molecular structure is uncertain and probabilistic, the outcome at the macroscopic level appears to be deterministic. If the universe was created with uncertainty as a necessity for physical objects to exist, then I wonder if everything is, in its very essence, uncertain. I've often heard well-intentioned people say that they know that they know that they know...*ad infinitum*... about some point of faith, be it the inerrancy of scripture, the death and resurrection of Jesus, or even the existence of God. It's as if they're trying to assure themselves that they are absolutely certain that all of these things are objectively true. The irony here is that if God created the universe with inherent, unescapable uncertainty down to the very structure of the atoms that make up all that is knowable to us using our five senses, then why would the spiritual realm be any different? I gather that Saint Paul was instructing the Roman church to let go of the need for certainty when he wrote that "Now hope that is seen is not hope. For who hopes for what is seen?"(Romans 8:24). Paul also says in one of his letters to the Corinthian church, "And now faith, hope, and love abide, these three...." (1 Corinthians 13:13)—a trinity of uncertainty, yes?

> The courage to act is rooted in faith, hope, and love, not certainty.

We have a desire to know. We crave certainty. Yet the only things that we know with any degree of certainty are things that have already happened. Prophecy can only be substantiated after the fact. Up to that point, there is always uncertainty. I believe that this is by divine design. No one should know the future because we would be paralyzed by that knowledge. The courage to act is rooted in faith, hope, and love, not certainty. A probabilistic future allows us to act according to our free will with the hope that, in the end, all will be redeemed. Saint Paul wrote these encouraging words to the Roman church, "We know that all things work together for good for those who love God, who are called according to his purpose" (Romans 8:28). This is perhaps, the most succinct statement in the Bible of the uncertainty of human agency moving toward a certain outcome.

An Invitation to Star-Gazing

Michael Andrews

Professor Michael F. Andrews is the McNerney-Hanson University Endowed Chair in Ethics and serves as the Dean of the College of Arts and Sciences and the director of the Reason, Ethics, and Faith Collaborative at the University of Portland. He has lectured and published widely in the areas of ethics, phenomenology, and Catholic intellectual thought, most recently at Oxford University, Loyola University of Chicago, and the state universities of Vienna and Cologne. He currently serves as Vice-President of the International Association of the Study of the Philosophy of Edith Stein.

I often remind my students that we risk forgetting Socrates' maxim that "the unexamined life is not worth living" at our own peril. Contemporary culture seems to have little patience for exploring deep, existential thinking beyond what can be explained in a convenient soundbite or television infomercial. I have been teaching philosophy for a quarter of a century, and I have served as a dean or academic program director for almost half that tIme. From myriad conversations with students and their families I have learned that the term "philosophy professor" conjures images of a well-intentioned yet absent-minded professor, an abstract theoretician who is so far removed from reality that the very idea of studying philosophy in a systematic or comprehensive fashion is usually met with disdain, derision, even downright hostility. Plato first described the "philosopher" as a person able to grasp what is eternal and unchangeable from what is merely opinion and perceptual conjecture. Ever since, the teaching of philosophy has remained an object of intense scorn and contempt, a box to "check" along the Grand Tour of General Education Requirements. In contemporary circles, philosophy has recently become equated with radical, subjective skepticism: my truths are mine and your truths are yours and there are, subsequently, as many truths as there are perspectives. Into such a non-sensical world of infinite variability, I imagine many people would rightfully expect the job of a philosophy professor to entail, at best, an impractical ability to teach the history of ideas or, as someone described in a recent op-ed attack against intellectual elitism in higher education, "the history of bullshit."

I suppose, to a certain extent, they are right. After all, most of the themes with which I engage students in a course titled "philosophy of the human person" or ethics or metaphysics or existentialism or "great figures"—Kierkegaard, Nietzsche, Thomas Aquinas, Spinoza, Edith Stein, Husserl—entail questions of ultimate concern. Who (or what) is God? What is justice? How does one live the good life? Does one have a soul and, if so, what difference does it make? What happens after death? I suppose questions of ultimate concern don't often make headlines, nor do they contribute to the Gross National Product, nor a comfortable 401k retirement plan. But they are questions that every man and woman of integrity faces, consciously or not, thematically or not, during his or her brief existence. Baruch Spinoza reminds us that all things excellent are as difficult as they are rare. This is what makes them questions of *ultimate* concern.

What do I really teach when I teach Philosophy? For one, I remind my students—and myself—that we live in a universe that was not made by human hands. Rather, we are made by it. Physics estimates the age of the universe to be approximately 13.8 billion years. There is nothing in the universe that is not also somehow intriguingly present in every molecule of human DNA. With an estimated *one billion trillion* stars in the observable universe, modern astronomers explain that life is rendered possible only on planets (such as Earth) that have evolved from gas born from third-generation neutron stars. Quite literally, we are made of stardust. Even more: through philosophy's conversations with mathematics, biology, physics, and chemistry, we are able to put the universe into our heads. Through imagination, the *universe comes to think about itself.* And when we think about ourselves thinking about ourselves, such conscious self-reflection typically means

> When we think about ourselves thinking about ourselves, such conscious self-reflection typically means we have more questions than we have answers.

we have more questions than we have answers.

As a philosophy professor, I do not teach any *thing*. When I teach philosophy I invite my students **to learn how to learn**; to learn how to live with deep existential insights; how to wrestle with difficult and uncomfortable thoughts; how to handle having more questions than answers; how to embrace intellectual honesty and personal integrity without having to rely on easy, ready-made answers to The Question of All Questions: *"Why is there something rather than nothing?"* We do not live in a world that naturally makes time for questions of ultimate concern. Instead, we collectively rush towards the accumulation of material comfort, deny the significance of transcendence, seek a creed that emphasizes radical self-fulfillment, and engage in acts of judgment and even violence against human beings whom, we often conveniently forget, are also created in the image of God.

Properly speaking, the subject matter of philosophy is love (*philo*) of wisdom (*sophia*). Through methods of rational discourse—including logic, critical thinking, ontology, ethics, epistemology, and metaphysics—philosophers through the ages have attempted to grapple with ways by which the pursuit of wisdom might actually be taught. In *Metaphysics,* for example, Aristotle notes that "all inquiry begins with wonder." And so, perhaps, the study of philosophy might best be described, at least in metaphysical terms, as an invitation to "wonder-seeking" or "star-gazing." Concepts such as "imagination" and "wonder" cannot be taught, but they can be cultivated. Real learning happens through practice and the process of change, what the Greeks called *meta-morphosis.* Consequently, the question, "Who am I?" is determined by what I love and the measure of such love. St. Augustine's exhortation to "love, and do as you will" necessitates that purity of heart means to will one thing. Even more: words like "mercy" and "imagination" and "truth" and "beauty" are not simply nouns but become verbs. The just man *justices,* as the Jesuit poet Gerard Manley Hopkins reminds us.

Some of the companions that I have met along my own philosophical journey include Plato, Augustine, and Thomas Aquinas, who acknowledge that beauty can be grasped only through anamnesis, or recollection; Spinoza, Anselm, and Locke, who joyfully celebrate the limitations of knowledge amidst the emergence of genuine transcendence; Kierkegaard, Whitman, and Nietzsche, who delve into the dizziness of freedom as antidote against the onslaught of social collectivity and mass homogenization; Derrida, Levinas, and Husserl, who believe everything that is constructible (which is everything) is also *de*-constructible. As a philosopher, I remind students that we are all foreigners in a strange land, refugees seeking Home in a universe that is at once beautiful and perplexing, immense yet particular. I help students come to terms with the limitations of their knowledge and the implications of what it means to not know. Such insight can be very disorienting, especially to those who require certainty that what they know is true, clear, and distinct. The philosophical life offers no such certainties. Our so-called "heroes" are those who seek wisdom in all its frailty and seek truth beyond comfort and convenience; those few individual seekers whose "desire and will revolve, like a wheel that is evenly moved, by the Love which moves the sun and the other stars," as Dante put it. Teaching philosophy oftentimes means learning how to persevere amidst outward uncertainty and inner transformation.

Part II

Connect

*"There are moments when the heart is generous,
and then it knows that for better or worse our lives are woven together here,
one with one another and with the place and all the living things."*—Wendell Berry, in Jayber Crow

Prologue

Shannon Mayer

…woven together here, one with one another…

Perhaps you have had the experience of feeling alone in a room full of people or of working hard to navigate a relationship that, for a season, left you feeling lonely and struggling to bond in a satisfying and meaningful way. What does it mean to be *with* one another? Connection isn't simply a matter of proximity. The act of truly being *with* another is a daring act. It takes intentionality, vulnerability, and at times even a bold fearlessness. It's chancy business, the act of *authentic* presence. Colleges and universities provide a unique (some say idyllic) setting in which authentic connection happens *every day*—little miracles encountered in a seemingly infinite number of creative and transformative ways. The teachers who authored the following essays explore what it means to connect…one *with* one another…through words, collective experiences, and the thoughtful exploration of our shared humanity.

Spelunking with A Dim Flashlight

Rev. Patrick Hannon, CSC

English Professor Fr. Patrick Hannon, CSC, is the author of four collections of essays. His most recent book is *Sacrament: Personal Encounters with Memories, Wounds, Dreams, and Unruly Hearts.*

I love words and the look of them, and how some of them sound in my head when I read them. I must confess, though, I prefer the Anglo-Saxon over the Latinate. I prefer an ax, for instance, not a hatchet. I prefer words with stubble on them, not the clean shaven kind. I love the smell of words, too, or at least the smell of the trade paper they're written on and the industrial ink that gives them life. I love when I stumble onto an unfamiliar word and then, after I look it up and become acquainted with it—after a bit of awkward courting, that is—it quite naturally gathers all its belongings and moves right in to that part of my brain where all my words live.

Sometime around the time my second-grade teacher showed me how to diagram a sentence, in a moment of anger I called my older brother a degenerate—a word I had apparently stumbled upon and fell in love with; and my brother—not knowing what the word meant but duly suspicious—punched me rather hard in the arm; and my mother, who as I remember it now was stifling a laugh, sent me to my room to cool off. It was then I discovered that words have power, that they were scrappy, brave, and loyal little troopers who could, if I used them well, help me defend myself—the runt of my particular litter—against a world that was, every day, becoming bigger and stronger than I would ever be.

Like our grandmother's finest china, we save some words, thankfully, for rare occasions, because otherwise they become unremarkable and pedestrian. *Hate* is one of those words for me, at least. But I fear the word *love*, used in a raw and honest way, might be one of those words, too. We began using *love* interchangeably with *like* years ago, when we stopped using words such as *nifty* and *keen* and *groovy*. I know I tend to overuse the word *love* in this attenuated form. An overly zealous wordsmith will occasionally call me on it when I say, "I love rocky road ice cream" or "I love Sierra Nevada Pale Ale" or "I love baseball." Okay. So I probably do overuse the word, but I still emphatically *love* words.

I love (there I go again) that some words can scare the bejesus out of you (side note: I love the word *bejesus*, a mild expletive of Irish origin) such as the phrase "I have something to tell you" or "You might want to sit down." And some words or strings of words (a "pearl necklace round the neck of poverty," the poet Patrick Kavanagh put it—he was referring to God but might have just as well been talking about words as far as I'm concerned) leave us so exposed and vulnerable that we might properly wonder how it is they get uttered at all, words such

as "Will you marry me?" or "I'm in love with you" or "Will you forgive me?"

I find it hopeful as a Catholic priest and a writer and a teacher of writing that in the Gospel of John we have no story of Jesus being born. Instead, John gives us his prologue which begins, "In the beginning was the Word, and the Word was with God, and the Word was God." I like the Spanish translation of that portion of John's prologue better, though. It says in the beginning was "El Verbo." In the beginning was "The Verb." And the Verb was with God, and the Verb was God. Something tells me the voice of that verb is not passive.

We've been speaking words a whole lot longer than we've been writing them down. I've often thought this was because we were too busy trying not to be some saber-toothed tiger's lunch to be sitting around musing with pen and paper. (Here I imagine with ironic pleasure the first ink pen, crafted around the sixth century from goose or turkey feathers, and how those plucked carcasses must have made for fine feasting after a day of writing.) But why did it take over three millennia (give or take a few centuries) after we had begun to brew beer (Mesopotamia, circa 5000 BCE, FYI), for instance, to begin writing down beautiful and haunting and lasting stories such as *The Epic of Gilgamesh,* a written work decidedly not tied to commerce and business?

I think now it's because we know in our gut that it is practically insane to write our stories down, when they and the sentences we use to construct them assume a life separate from our own, even as they owe their existence to us. They become, in other words, our children. And we writers love them almost as much as their fleshy counterparts. And the thought that one of our written stories or poems or essays or screenplays will be dismissed as ugly or idiotic or silly or an abject failure or, God forbid, mediocre will often leave us staring at a blank page or computer screen for days. We pause—sometimes for years—at the thought of creating something we think is beautiful that will, in the end and forever, be teased and bullied. Equally horrifying is the awful truth that if rejection does happen we will be helpless to stop it.

And yet we write prose and poetry anyway.

> I think writing—truthful, tinged with doubt, brave, and sustained by foolish desire—is as close to God as we writers can get, and that is a scary thought indeed.

I tell my students on the first day of a new semester that essay writing is not about following the rules of grammar and punctuation. It's not about crafting safe sentences and paragraphs. It's about taking ridiculous risks. It's spelunking into deep dark caves with a very dim flashlight. It's walking a tightrope without a safety net. I think writing—truthful, tinged with doubt, brave, and sustained by foolish desire—is as close to God as we writers can get, and that is a scary thought indeed. Because in the end, this holy ambition will draw us too close to the fire. And this encounter with the flaming Word will burn layers and layers off of us. And then, like God, we will be utterly fearless, utterly exposed.

And we will know something of the pain of joy.

Sophrosyne

Lauretta Frederking

Political Science Professor Lauretta Frederking received the University of Portland's award for outstanding scholarship in 2012. She is author of the book *Economic and Political Integration in Immigrant Neighborhoods: Trajectories of Virtuous and Vicious Cycles* and editor of the book *Hemingway on Politics and Rebellion.*

My richest learning and teaching haven't happened in the classroom and not so much in the formal places of intellectual exchange. What I really teach has happened at those in-between places, the falling-down moments when I purposely shed my expertise. Yes, what I really teach seems to have happened when I am not teaching at all, just living a relationship of communion with students.

A few years ago I was introduced to the word *sophrosyne*. There is no precise translation of the Greek word into English. Really it can be explained only by a run of complexities, a balance of contraries such as: success and failure are equal imposters (triumph and disaster according to Rudyard Kipling); everything matters for who we may be *becoming* and simultaneously nothing matters in terms of who we *are*. When I am pressed, sophrosyne can be described with simplicity as "temperance" or "wisdom," though neither noun fully captures the word's essence. Sophrosyne is what I teach students during in-between places and falling-down moments, when things are often not as they appear on the surface. Be cautious with good news because it may not be what you hoped for, I tell them, and be open to bad news because it may be the first carving out of a path of self-discovery.

I remember the long arc back to my college years when life appeared in binary terms—success/failure, acceptance/rejection, love/loss—and I vividly recall the stings and ecstasies of both. I see that similar disposition in students. A 'C' ruins them, a heartbreak destroys all future possibilities of happiness; and then, on the other track, an 'A' glorifies them, and a triumph affirms their superstardom destiny. I try to be the sandpaper that reminds them an 'A' is a challenge, just as a 'C/D/F' may be an opportunity. Success and failure are equal imposters.

Most often, this teaching happens outside the classroom. One of my students came to me in the process and then the final stage of being dismissed from the university. He was devastated and also entirely to blame for the actions that led to his dismissal. I assured him that this might be the most defining moment of his life, not at all because of its failure but because of its potential. "This could be the moment when you discover who you want to be and not be. Seize it. Wallow in it. But don't ever forget that life is long enough and God's grace is powerful enough that this horrible moment may be your great opportunity."

> I trust that each student carries the experiences and conversations and moments of reflection with them. Grace rarely happens in an expected way.

I have caught more than one student in the midst of cheating on a quiz, a test, an assignment. Certainly the university has a protocol for cheating. However, more important than the administrative steps, I ask a student if he/she is a cheater. Almost always, they respond "no," "no way," "this was an accident," "I made a mistake." My response is simple and always the same. If you cheat, you become a cheater. If you aren't a cheater, don't cheat, not even once. This is your time to figure out who you are. Let me know when you have figured it out. Often I see the outcome. He or she declares the turnaround to never cheat again, and they don't. I believe them. Sometimes there is silence, or the student drops out of the class. While troubling to me, maybe those students have figured out who they are as well. I trust that our students' roads extend beyond their time in higher education and that each student carries the experiences and conversations and moments of reflection with them. Grace rarely happens in an expected way.

I remember another student appeared during office hours and asked for a letter of recommendation. She had received an 'A' in a course I taught her the previous semester and wanted to apply for graduate school. I told her that I knew nothing about her beyond her 'A' and asked her to share with me why she wanted to get into the particular program. She couldn't answer beyond her hard-driving, achievement-oriented sensibilities that she thought it would be good for her career. "But why do you want that career?' at which point I could see her cheeks redden. She stammered in a way that suggested great offense. She reminded me that she had received an 'A' in my class. I asked her to think about my question and come back to me when she had an answer. I still don't know exactly what she was feeling at the time, but I do know that around and beyond her irritation she came to realize she needed to be able to answer that question for herself before she pursued the next stage of her academic life.

Colleges and universities invite students and professors into relationship. I accept that a lot of my job is sharing information and expertise. But I realize there have been students who, for whatever reason or spiritual mystery, reached out in a way that invited me into being part of their life journey, figuring out who they were right be-fore my eyes. We teachers can keep it clean and transactional—you give me a paper and I give you a grade—or we can open it up to be a potentially meaningful place of growth. In so many ways, our students come to us socially hard-wired to think like strategic calculators when it comes to teachers and academic environments. I want to tear down that assumption. Teaching is more than being the most learned person in the room. Being there when students are overcoming adversity and penetrating their authentic purpose puts us teachers at the center of who they are and what they will bring to the world. I hope my students all have many successes and many failures—not to learn how to avoid the latter and win more of the former but rather to learn that who they are is the same good and growing person regardless of what "grade" society gives them. Living from a place of who we are, less driven by illusions or expectations of where we think we need to be going, takes practice. Higher education often provides a safe place to figure that out. Sophrosyne.

Learning to *SHUT UP*

Jeff Kerssen-Griep

Communication Professor Jeff Kerssen-Griep studies intercultural communication phenomena important to feedback and instruction, helping teachers shape skilled classroom interactions, engaged learning environments, and intrinsically motivated learning. He has received the University of Portland's outstanding teaching (2004) and scholarship (2010) awards and in 2006 was designated a "Master Teacher" by his disciplinary colleagues.

Teaching is an unnatural act, an incursion on another person's learning-in-progress: it's a yippy little dog, a surprise water balloon, a telemarketer on a sunny day. Each persuasive attempt to get students learning about barium or facework or Hegel or genderlects or sine waves or Afghanistan comes with a built-in demand that they stop thinking—for a while—about what yesterday's unexpected smile really meant, or why mom and dad are divorcing, or lunch. It's a challenge for me to teach while suspecting my students may cast my dignified self as a water-fighting sales terrier, but teaching is no doubt an imposition, a sustained redirection of other curious creatures' voracious cogitation. In the sport of curling terms, students are sentient rocks slowly cruising; I push/glide/sweep my way alongside and a little ahead, strategically melting patches of frigid path, aiming for productive "clicks" at the end of things.

I am Teacher; hear me impose. This presents a daily dilemma not easily resolved: research shows us that students' purest motivations and richest learnings emerge best when we impose least, when they're given as much autonomy as we can muster during the process—especially given USAmericans' "don't fence me in" prickliness about being told what to do. This is an uncomfortable truth for those of us called to smart 'em up, since each course's learning objectives lasso students' otherwise free-ranging interests.

How do I direct without dictating? Even better, how can I teach in ways that help them fall in love with seeking?

Okay, in truth, sometimes I just cop out and dictate (ab-dictate?). Teachers, like ranchers and nations, sometimes wave off the gnatty and knotty realities of imposition and simply pull rank to get others looking and sounding like we think they should. For example, sometimes I find myself not-so-slyly corralling what happens in class by talking *at* my students, who diligently write my stuff down. I'm not alone in this, mind you. Like most of us, I was socialized to believe that "teaching" equaled "telling." There's the story of a new dean who, after twenty minutes watching an experienced professor facilitate small groups expertly working on a problem, sidled up to whisper that he would come back to observe on a day when the professor was "actually teaching." That's been a powerful addiction for verboso-me to kick: the teach/tell/talking belief that defines "learning" as "students memorizing my understandings" instead of constructing their own. It resembles belching in its effects— satisfying for manufacturer, but less so for belchees.

> Tending those pesky teacher-learner relationships is at the unavoidable heart of our work.

What are the costs of mere exhaling? Students' love of learning can wither, and they often come to resent their teachers' authority (and the things teachers value, like fresh ideas), just as citizens of occupied countries look askance at their overseers' virtues. Teaching as an occupation, indeed. Nor does abdicating one's rank and course goals to curry students' friendship bring anything more than a new set of problems.

But yea, though I have walked through the noisome valley of teaching-is-all-about-me, there is another path—a co-creation, a dialectic/dialogic practice of building new knowledge and relationships by exhaling and inhaling *with* our ever-learning students. Tending those pesky teacher-learner relationships is at the unavoidable heart of our work. We negotiate them in the guise of messages about due dates and design logistics and weekend assignments and paper topics.

One memorable early experience of such a parley involved trying to re-collect an exam failed by Jon, a charismatic, disturbed, sweet, and lousy student. He refused to give back his test, on which were questions

I was charged with keeping secret for other teaching assistants to use. Jon trumpeted to the class that he had done so poorly he was too ashamed to let me have his test back. When I (young and foolish) tried to grab it from him, his face lit up as his bug-eyed classmates held their collective breath, and we knew he had me. After class, I stopped talking *at* him:

Me: *"So…what's the deal here?"*

He: *"My samurai self is too shamed by this performance; I won't be able to show myself at synagogue. I can't let anyone see this ever again."*

Me: *"Well—that's what I want, too…what should we do?"*

He: *"Can we burn it?"*

Thus did we find ourselves seated side-by-side on brick steps, briefly parting the puzzled river of incoming students with a torched test and secret smiles.

Felicitous classroom relationships also change what we learn, morphing us from mainframes to mentors in the process. A novice teacher in class once challenged my claim that all teaching is values-laden. I asked Aimee her favorite book to use with her kindergarteners (*Goodnight Moon*), we queried the "moral" of that story (peace, calm care, and ever-present love), then asked whether she gave angst, hate, and indifference equal time in her class. Those two minutes were an epiphany for all of us, and they'd arisen from conversation, not lecture.

One good colleague argues that most of the time we don't talk our way into good relationships, we listen our way into them, one conversation at a time. This is always a challenge where there's a built-in power difference, even more so if I just can't shut up—but I know by now that I earn more genuine influence over my students' learning by judiciously giving up some control over how they get to epiphany. Though I shiver a bit as I floss my ears and prepare to dance with my students each teaching day, I'm convinced that responsive-yet-goal-focused guidance is best for their learning, for them, for us, and for me. Healthy relations need room to breathe, so to give my students air I'm learning to shut up. And perhaps it's time I do that now.

Language at the Outer Edge of Longing

Laura McLary

German Professor Laura McLary is the 2015 CASE Carnegie Oregon Professor of the Year. Her publications on twentieth-and-twenty-first-century Austrian literature and culture include the book *Winning Back Lost Territory: The Writing of Lilian Faschinger* (written and co-edited with Vincent Kling). She is currently working on a book on the Austrian poet Georg Trakl.

"God speaks to each of us before he makes us."—Rainer Maria Rilke

*W*enn Sie diesen Satz sehen, denken Sie vielleicht, dass Deutsch eine unschöne Sprache ist. But maybe you would use a different term: muscular, harsh, aggressive. I've heard it all: German is ugly, it's irrelevant, it's only good for shouting and cursing. And that's precisely why I teach German. For a variety of important historical reasons, German has a complicated reputation, but it is possible to engage with those historical reasons and look for nuance. It is possible to get beyond the culturally accepted stereotype in American culture of the German language and German-speaking cultures. It is possible to learn that all languages, all cultures, have the capacity for expressing the full range of emotions and experiences that belong to the human family.

When I was a high school student in Ohio, I decided to study German because I wanted a way to gain access to a broader world. My parents helped to cultivate in me a curiosity about people and places all around the world. My father traveled frequently around the world for his work and brought home stories and pictures of his international experiences. My mother was a social worker, and for her it was important to instill into my siblings and me respect for everyone, especially those living at the margins of our society. For Christmas one year, she gave me James Baldwin's *If Beale Street*

Could Talk, Chaim Potok's *The Chosen,* and William Lederer and Eugene Burdick's *The Ugly American.* My first reaction to these gifts was: What do these books have to do with me? But as I read, I came to identify with the struggles of the protagonists whose cultures were so different from my own. It made sense to me, to my very core, that the perspective of white US-America wasn't the only way to see the world. And I started reading English translations of German like Günter Grass's *The Tin Drum* and Herman Hesse's *Der Steppenwolf.* Grass's unreliable narrator and Hesse's psychically torn main character led me down a twisting, dark tunnel of ambiguity and double-entendre that seemed custom-made for my teenaged questioning about identity, history, and the role of truth.

Reading was a way for me to access different voices, and studying German seemed like a logical extension of that line of inquiry. When I was an undergraduate student, I had the opportunity to study abroad in Salzburg, Austria. I couldn't imagine a life at that point that didn't include German. Eventually, German Studies became for me a way to connect deeply with my experiences studying abroad in Austria. I fell in love with the ambiguities of the culture, especially its strong literary and arts tradition.

I live inside German, and I love the language and its flexibility and expressiveness. I yearn for its vibrant, gorgeous literary and artistic traditions, represented by a diversity of voices and experiences today and over time.

German-speaking culture is an access point for working with students on all kinds of important issues and skills. We practice becoming more adept readers and writers, and we learn about recurring motifs in German-speaking cultures that are expressed through literature, art, film, non-fiction writing, and social and historical developments. My students and I can always find access points through German that connect with current global issues and concerns: environmental degradation, inequality, and—always—our ongoing search for meaning and connection. While we are working on mastering the dative case and musing over why German nouns are assigned one of three genders, we are really working on finding our way around in an unfamiliar and perhaps uncomfortable space. The more we practice that discomfort, the more we can set ourselves on a path toward becoming thoughtful, compassionate, and effective global citizens.

As an academic discipline, the study of German

or any other foreign language aligns perfectly with the mission of higher education. We want our students to become highly literate readers and writers who can reflect on the role of language and culture as it shapes our own *Weltanschauung*. As an academic discipline *and* as a shaper of values, the study of German or any other foreign language provides students with access to understanding a diversity of people from around the world. My most fervent wish as an educator is that students will leave my classes with a strong basis for living and working successfully in a German-speaking country and that as a result they will encounter with an open heart other cultures and languages that might be significantly different from their own.

Language is a poignant expression of what makes us human. When we experience the discomfort of trying on a foreign language, we grow and become acutely aware of our interdependence with other people and places. Students who pursue deep study of a foreign language are more aware of their own cultural beliefs and consequently become more comfortable living, thinking, and working in the spaces between cultures. They bring more compassion and understanding to their relationships with people from different cultures and seek out ways to bridge differences in a world that is increasingly interconnected. They live in a new space that is richly textured with the full range of human emotions and experiences. German stops sounding or looking foreign and a bit intimidating; it becomes another way to express an opinion or a feeling, to organize an idea, or to find a solution to a problem that might not exist in one's native language.

Recently, a former student sent me the gift of a poem he had heard, entitled "Wincing at the Beautiful" by Paul Hostovsky. In the poem, there is a reference to a poem by the Austrian poet Rainer Maria Rilke, and that sent me on a search to find Rilke's own words, *"Gott spricht zu jedem nur, eh er ihn macht"* ("God Speaks to Each of Us Before He Makes Us"). It is a prayer of sorts, a prayer that God

> My most fervent wish as an educator is that students will encounter with an open heart other cultures and languages that might be significantly different from their own.

speaks to each one of us before we are made, that urges us to enter the "land called life," to embrace both "beauty and terror," to live on "longing's outer edge," to hold God's hand and experience the full range of human emotions. This is what *all* languages do. They breathe life. They give voice to our deepest desires. They give praise. They connect us all.

Gott spricht zu jedem nur, eh er ihn macht (1899)
Rainer Maria Rilke

Gott spricht zu jedem nur, eh er ihn macht,
dann geht er schweigend mit ihm aus der Nacht.
Aber die Worte, eh jeder beginnt,
diese wolkigen Worte, sind:

Von deinen Sinnen hinausgesandt,
geh bis an deiner Sehnsucht Rand;
gib mir Gewand.

Hinter den Dingen wachse als Brand,
dass ihre Schatten, ausgespannt,
immer mich ganz bedecken.

Lass dir Alles geschehn: Schönheit und Schrecken.
Man muss nur gehn: Kein Gefühl ist das fernste.
Lass dich von mir nicht trennen.
Nah ist das Land,
das sie das Leben nennen.

Du wirst es erkennen
an seinem Ernste.

Gib mir die Hand.

God Speaks to Each of Us Before He Makes Us
Rainer Maria Rilke

God speaks to each of us before he makes us,
then from the dark he walks with us in silence.
But the words, before we each begin,
These cloudy words, he speaks:

Sent out by your senses,
go up to your longing's outer edge;
give me raiment.

Behind the things, grow as a flame,
whose shadows over me unfurl,
always cloaking me entire.

Let all things happen to you: beauty and terror.
You must but go: No feeling is too far-flung.
Let us never be apart.
Near is the land
that they call life.

You will know it
by its earnest zeal.

Give me your hand.

         Translation by Laura McLary, 2016

The Many Facets of Humanness

Anissa Rogers

Professor of Social Work Anissa Rogers has interests in the intersections of aging, gender, sexuality, mental health, and end-of-life issues. She is the recipient of the prestigious Hartford grant and contributes to national social work education policy. She is the author of the textbook, *Human Behavior in the Social Environment*, and maintains a clinical counseling practice.

Social work is messy. It is messy because human beings are messy. And with messiness comes complexity. Many people, including some of our students, think social workers are "those people who take away other people's kids." While serving children who are abused and neglected can be part of what social workers do, our work involves so much more. To be effective social workers, we must have a wide knowledge base in many disciplines such as biology, psychology, politics, and economics that help us conceptualize why problems happen and what to do about them. But we also must grasp the nuanced interplay of dynamic social, cultural, political, historical, economic, spiritual, psychological, and interpersonal forces that shape who we are, the problems we face, and our individual and collective responses to those problems. Given human nature—and the way it is reflected in our culture and social institutions—unpacking, analyzing, and working with it can be dizzyingly complicated and very messy.

The social work profession is founded on ethical principles that promote values such as service, integrity, competence, social justice, the dignity and worth of the person, and the importance of human relationships. It seeks to understand how our social and institutional structures undermine and support these values as well as human potential for self-actualization. Often the values of social work are pitted against the realities of human situations, bringing ethical dilemmas that can also be very messy.

It is this complexity, and the messiness that accompanies it, that I *really* teach. Of course I go to great lengths to ensure that students are exposed to the language, theories, methods, approaches, and knowledge of the field. As much as possible, I help students understand the connections social work has to other disciplines and why those connections are crucial to our work. But underpinning the content related to knowledge and my approach to teaching is the goal of exposing students to the multifaceted nature of social work. Sometimes it means showing students the underbelly of the work they will be doing, including asking students to explore old wounds and focusing on the tragedies of the human condition. But it also means teaching the opportunities, successes, and gratification students are sure to experience as they help transform individual lives, families, and communities. Most importantly, it is about helping students figure out how to hold on to hope and persevere in the face of the hope-

> **How do I help students be with and respond to the suffering of others without feeling swallowed or paralyzed by it?**

lessness and helplessness they will feel at times.

Every day, questions like these cross my mind: How do I approach teaching about the nature of social work and its complexity? How do I help students learn about social institutions that, while constructed to help, often undermine the human spirit and perpetuate poverty, discrimination, oppression, and hopelessness? How do I instill hope in students that they can be change agents in systems that sometimes lose sight of their purposes and goals? How do I help students develop and connect with their compassion and empathy, especially when this can seem scary or overwhelming? How do I help students be with and respond to the suffering of others without feeling swallowed or paralyzed by it?

The way I try to answer these questions for myself and my teaching often comes back to what it means to be human with both our *light* and *shadow* sides. This includes our potential to be simultaneously kind, giving, benevolent, and compassionate as well as hateful, uncaring, selfish, and thoughtless. To help us all grapple with this, I want my students to develop a safe place to explore the many facets of humanness. Students need to become self-reflective, analytical thinkers who can challenge their own and others' biases and stereotypes that can breed hatred, rigidity, intolerance, prejudice, and a lack of creativity in response to problems. I help students explore the boundless possibilities in human potential to bring goodness and joy to the world. An important concept for students to learn is how the power of individual experiences helps to shape worldviews. Students must learn to own their experiences while allowing others to own theirs. It is from this understanding that we can move forward to make change.

Teaching for me is about exposing students to new ideas that shake up and transform their worldviews, while helping them listen more carefully to—and sometimes shake up—the worldviews of others. Teaching is about helping students challenge what they think they know and find human connection in a collective experience. It is about helping students find ways to remain curious and reduce blaming and scapegoating, which can leave many students wondering, "What can *I* do? I'm only one person!" In addition to being "doers," students need to learn to be silent, reflective, insightful, and able to sit with others in the midst of struggle. In a world that is quick to assume, pass judgment, and jump to fix things, one of the most difficult things I try to help students learn is to quiet these urges so they can be authentically present with people in the moment. I demonstrate how such presence can lead to greater understanding, healing, and discernment about how and when to act.

Learning and practicing presence takes a tremendous amount of courage on the part of students. To me, teaching is about providing a companion on that journey. Part of social work, and therefore my job as a teacher and co-learner, is allowing the messiness of human life to unfold and not be intimidated by it. Sometimes the mess happens on its own, but sometimes we need to help people find the courage to make that mess before we can help to *sort it out* and *clean it up*.

Everything *Always* Has a Past

Christin Hancock

History Professor Christin Hancock studies the intersections of gender, race, and health in the modern American past. She has published her work in a number of historical journals, including the *Journal of Women's History*. She also serves on the editorial advisory board of the *Oregon Historical Quarterly*, Oregon's peer-reviewed public history journal.

In the late summer of 2014, Ferguson, Missouri, and then the nation, erupted in protest over yet another police killing of an unarmed black youth, Michael Brown. For some, the protests seemed to come out of nowhere. For others the protests became illegitimate the moment the Department of Justice determined the police officer involved to be justified in his actions. As a scholar of gender and race in American history, I, like other scholars in my field, immediately recognized the connections between this individual story and the much larger legacy of U.S. racial history. In fact, this was not an individual story; it never could be. It was, and is, always embedded in the complicated, tragic, and painful story of American constructions of race and racism. Such is the case with nearly every social, political, and economic event that occurs in our present. Everything always has a past.

The growing national movement inspired by the Ferguson protests (as well as the systemic violence against unarmed black men that had inspired it and continues to fuel it) has become a guiding focus of our collective historical inquiry in my course in African American History. Students use the historical method and historical inquiry to help them engage with and make sense of the pressing questions about race and racism in our contemporary world. Through historical inquiry, students learn to move beyond anecdotes and personal experiences to understand issues of power and inequality in a broader historical context. Once they begin this process, they are often surprised by their own shifts in thinking.

Students often begin their inquiry believing that history is the study of the true past. Some students anticipate that history will be boring and irrelevant, a tiresome list of dates and names and wars and presidents, but boredom aside they assume with certainty that there is an explicit and resolute truth to it. They believe that the past can be quantified and organized and expressed, much like a mathematical equation, in a way that reveals absolute truth.

Historians by contrast know that history is alive, dynamic, ever-changing. We look into the past with hopes of pinning down words, remembrances, pictures, feelings, experiences, and ever-shifting numbers, all of which sometimes present conflicting realities. Our task is to collect all of these moving parts, hold them still long enough to reveal a usable shape, and find some order to the collection. We critique, we interpret, and we shape our gathered kitsch into narratives that we hope bring some order to our collective understanding of the past.

Past President of the American Historical Association, Peter Stearns, has written that history "harbors beauty."[1] And it can. It can help us discover beauty in many realms, not the least of which is the way that human beings have built and sustained relationships that create good in the world. History can also, however, uncover a terrible ugliness—one that sometimes leads to beauty, but not necessarily. As a social historian, one who studies the lives of those who have often been marginalized in American society and culture, I deal with both the ugliness and the beauty of the American past. One of my favorite historians, Gerda Lerner, claims that only a people who possess a past have the capacity to imagine a future.[2] Thus history becomes an essential ingredient in, and a precursor for, positive social change. Our willingness to engage the past influences the present.

In teaching American social history, I'm not only teaching my students the historical method and historical content, but I'm also teaching ethics. I teach students to recognize power and inequality in the past and follow those threads into the present. I ask them to make connections between the past and the present and to allow that historical context to help inform their understandings of truth and justice.

Although I generally don't teach directly about current events, I do encourage students to think historically about important events that are happening to and around them. I want them to understand that history, like life itself, is filled with competing "truths." Often, students arrive in a history class assuming that they will be asked to memorize important dates and figures. But, as my dissertation advisor and McArthur Genius Award winner, Dr. Mari Jo Buhle, once said, "Dates and facts are handy things to have at your disposal. But they are not history."[3] By contrast, history is the process of sifting through historical documents, texts, and artifacts, analyzing them within their context and constructing usable narratives based on that analysis to help us make sense of the past. When I teach history, I am really asking my students to read. I am asking them to think critically about that which they read. And I am asking them to take a stand, construct a position, and make a case for the truth as they understand it.

> When I teach history, I am really asking my students to read. I am asking them to think critically about that which they read. And I am asking them to take a stand, construct a position, and make a case for the truth as they understand it.

The study of history is filled with competing truths. Historians rarely fully agree on their interpretations of the past. Engaging with these varied arguments helps students to understand themselves, who they are, and what they believe. It also asks students to recognize that, as the famous social historian Howard Zinn once wrote, "You can't be neutral on a moving train." Comfortable or not, I teach students to engage with a complicated and often deeply painful past—one that engages the way that race and gender have been constructed over time in the United States—and to take a stand. You can't remain neutral in my classes. I teach students ethics and compassion. I teach them to view the past not only through their own experience and personal lenses but also through the eyes of others who may or may not be like them. And then having viewed these multiple pasts, students must decide where they stand and how that stand requires them to live in the present. In the process of making those decisions, students learn to think not only critically but also ethically and, I hope, compassionately. Students learn that every current story has a past and that engaging with that past in a thoughtful, nuanced, and authentic way illuminates the present.

1. Peter Stearns, "Why Study History," Presidential Address to the American Historical Association, 1998.

2. Gerda Lerner, *Why History Matters: Thought and Life,* (Oxford University Press, 1998).

3. This is my paraphrasing of her words from a seminar in 1999 at Brown University.

Part III

Thrive

*"The nation doesn't simply need what we have,
it needs what we are."—St. Teresa Benedicta of the Cross (Edith Stein)*

Prologue

Jacquie Van Hoomissen

There is something inside each of us that seeks the new and the unknown. Sometimes we pursue it with unyielding passion, never wavering until we satisfy our curiosity. Other times we pause, unsure of which way to turn, pondering too much with too little action, and the opportunity slides past us like a wisp of wind in the spring moving on to a new meadow. Yet we remain a species driven by an innate curiosity about the world that propels us to action. We are fueled by a sense of yearning for more, a dissonance between where we are and where we would like to be. In essence, we become uneasy with how things are, which sometimes prompts us to change—either for good or for ill. The following essays by teachers in various disciplines of higher education describe what it is like to leave our state of comfort in order to grow. Through growth we can change, live to our full potential, and thrive as the human race.

The Flourishing of Every Soul

Karen E. Eifler

Education Professor Karen E. Eifler was the Carnegie Foundation Oregon Professor of the Year in 2006 and received the University of Portland's award for outstanding teaching in 2000. She is the editor of *Becoming Beholders: Cultivating sacramental imagination and action in college classrooms* and author of *A Month of Mondays: Spiritual Lessons from the Catholic Classroom.* Dr. Eifler is the co-director of the Garaventa Center of Catholic Intellectual Life and American Culture at the University of Portland.

I was on a windswept hill in Granada, Spain, when I figured out what I really teach. I was a week into a sabbatical that was supposed to be about learning enough Spanish to help my own Education students be effective teachers for the fastest growing language group in the state. I'd arrived able to count to ten and name all the colors in a box of crayons the size family restaurants give away: fourteen words. I also landed brimming with confidence about mastering Spanish, and why wouldn't I, with a lifetime GPA of 3.97, several diplomas on the wall back home, and genuine zeal for the project fueling me? So what if my placement test channeled me into the sub-slag of Level 1-A, for rock-bottom newcomers? I was there to learn, and so far I was the kind of student educators yearn for: all homework completed, meaningful eye contact made with both teachers in the two intensive courses I was taking each day, hand up to volunteer anytime it looked like participation was called for. I was even venturing out to a café each morning on my way to class in order to pick up an espresso for myself (in Spanish, it's also called "espresso"!) to begin building my fluency with practical applications of my new tongue.

There I was in an orange grove at the Alhambra, a royal complex that is among humanity's grandest accomplishments: lush gardens that bloom thanks to an ingenious medieval plumbing system that defies the high desert, mosaics that confound and dazzle the eyes, a palpable history of victories and travesties and complexities. I reach for a thesaurus even to describe it in my first language, it's so gobsmackingly resplendent. All this pulses through my mind when the teacher guiding our field trip asks what I think of this jewel in her nation's crown. I yearn—genuinely yearn—to communicate the awe, wonder, and gratitude I am feeling, and what comes out—offered here in literal translation is "Me think Alhambra much big and much pretty."

As a person who makes a living via language, I was horrified at the inadequacy of my words, never mind their assault on rudimentary grammar. I was exerting maximum effort, I'd eaten a full breakfast, I'd had two loving parents as a child, all the conditions dictated by conventional wisdom, politicians, the pope, and op-ed writers were in place for me to achieve basic verbal proficiency. And yet I sounded like a cavewoman when I was trying, oh so hard, to express myself in this new language. That's when it hit me that my sabbatical project wasn't about learning Span-

> I was there to experience what it's like to stagger uphill all day long as a learner and still have nothing to show for it, which is what an awful lot of kids in our schools today do.

ish at all. I was there to experience what it's like to stagger uphill all day long as a learner and still have nothing to show for it, which is what an awful lot of kids in our schools today do, the same schools for which I prepare young teachers to teach. My Neanderthal utterance was mortifying to me because it was such an anomaly in my regular existence, but my embarrassment would soon pass when I poured out my articulate thoughts in emails home to family and friends. I would feel competent again within an hour. But that's not how struggling learners experience the world of school. Even the most resilient child, I was stunned to realize in a graced flash of insight, has nothing like my reservoir of past academic successes to clamber for as a lifeline as they drown in unfamiliar squiggles and commands that seem to make sense to all the other kids in the room.

I teach courses in educational psychology, assessment, and classroom management. I can explain Vygotsky's pivotal notion of the Zone of Proximal Development seventeen different ways if necessary, but it occurred to me in the aftermath of that moment in the Alhambra that what I really teach, when I'm really teaching well, is *empathy*. I teach teachers, professionals who must be committed to the flourishing of every soul who walks through their door. And the starting point to helping others flourish, whether kindergarteners or AP Physics students, is empathy.

Most students don't answer a question immediately when it's posed in class. Did they not understand the question because the concept is unclear or because the language is still new? Did they not hear me because of an auditory problem? Have they eaten in the last twenty-four hours? Does a speech impediment make public responses a minor hell? Is their mind wandering to where they will be sleeping that night because the voucher for the family shelter expired? Are they worried they'll be branded a nerd for answering? In educational psychology, we are drilled to allow at least four seconds of wait-time after every question. This allows learners' brains to process the question, retrieve a solution from long-term memory, recall the protocols of a given classroom culture for speaking aloud. Do we raise hands or just call out? Do we answer in complete sentences or bullet points? That's a lot of cognitive work. But the four-second rule assumes everything else works: that the student isn't squirming with anxiety about mere decoding of the words pouring out of the teacher, or embarrassed to be showing lack of language skills or academic prowess, or scandalized by the realization that every other hand is up and *why, why, why do I not get this stuff?*

Empathy nudges me to sidle inside another's mind and heart and see what it's like in there, even to glimpse what I look and sound like from within that other world. Empathy turns a teacher's "how are you doing today?" into a genuine moment of human-to-human connection. Empathy has seared into me the awareness that a clumsy, stumbling response from a student can mask lava flows of perception and grateful appreciation, and knowing there was nothing I could do to remove the mask made the feeling of inadequacy exponentially worse. Every knowing begins with a not-knowing, and what I really teach teachers—gently, I hope—is to start their careful preparations by remembering what that feeling feels like.

The Ham Sandwich Theorem and Other Adventures in Persistence

Valerie Peterson

Mathematics Professor Valerie Peterson enjoys spreading research time among projects in topology, geometric group theory, and mathematics education. She is an advocate for and practitioner of inquiry-oriented pedagogy in undergraduate mathematics. Her work has appeared in math, applied math, and education journals.

Apparently, I am the kind of person you want to talk to on an airplane. I don't know why exactly—perhaps it is because I make eye contact and smile as I take my seat or simply because I tend to be device-less and headphone-free—but strangers seem compelled to strike up a conversation as we buckle up. At least, that is, until they inquire what I do for a living and I announce: "I teach math!" I love my job, so there is always an exclamation point here, but my enthusiasm rarely prevents the stricken, anxious look on my airplane neighbor's face. I don't take this personally—math phobia is widespread, often the result of lamentable early encounters with a subject regularly mistaken for (and taught as) a dry, black-and-white, skills-and-drills endeavor. I do, however, aspire to broaden and enrich others' views on the subject. I could reply, "I teach students to be persistent and adventurous, to think logically and critically, to develop the skills and habits of mind that *I* gained from years of studying math!" This is cumbersome (maybe even a bit obnoxious), but it certainly gets closer to the heart of what I do as a math professor.

To hint at the richness concealed in the simple phrase, "I teach math," I am obliged to begin with some of the traits and tools I developed as a result of doing a whole lot of math myself. Contrary to what you might expect of someone in my career, I have never been "good" at math in the culturally held sense. I'm not a whiz or genius. I'm slow at arithmetic; cannot perform complex, multi-step computations in my head; and have never been someone who looks at a math problem and simply "gets it." Quite the contrary, math for me has been an endeavor in endurance, an outlet for indulging my most stubborn and headstrong self, a one-foot-in-front-of-the-other campaign of utter persistence.

The adventure began in seventh grade, when I first bumped up against my intellectual ceiling in Mr. Sharp's algebra class. I found algebra confusing and frustrating. I didn't understand how to apply what I had seen in class to unfamiliar contexts in homework, and starting new problems was a mystery. My early assignments were turned in guiltily, full of mistakes and omissions, yet were handed back with notes of encouragement, indications of where I'd gone astray, and offers of help. If Mr. Sharp believed I could learn algebra, then perhaps I could. I redoubled my efforts, put in more time, and got extra help. It worked. I improved. I saw the results that hard work produced and felt the thrill of understanding something that once eluded me. I was hooked! After that, math still didn't come easily, but that became part of its appeal.

The rewards grew more profound over time. With every addition to my mathematical toolkit, I was ready for new levels of abstraction. In college calculus, I learned how to prove that my friend Ed *must* have been speeding at some point during his eighty-two-minute, one-hundred-mile drive from Santa Clara to Sacramento, even though he was never caught in the act.[1] In graduate school, I delighted in theorems that transformed the utterly theoretical back into the tangible. Take the Ham Sandwich Theorem in topology, which declares that a sandwich can be divided with one straight cut so that each half contains exactly the same volume of bread, meat, and cheese (this sounds intuitive until you try it with an n-dimensional sandwich for some $n > 3$). Differential geometry introduced the Hairy Ball Theorem[2]: every smooth vector field on a sphere has a singular point. That is, you can't comb flat the hair on a coconut without creating a cowlick. (Do try this at home!)

Beyond nerdy conversation starters for cocktail parties, math endowed me with qualities and habits of mind that fundamentally shape who I am and how I interact with the world. The arguments I form in everyday discourse are guided by the logical principles that underlie all mathematical reasoning. The ways in which I frame and present my thoughts, structure content for my classes, and even compose my shopping list are all influenced by the brevity and rigor I practice every time I write a mathematical proof. Doing math has taught me to ask, and answer, meaningful questions, to break down a statement into its foundational parts, and to put together many small pieces to build up new truths.

It is not only structure and precision that I've gained from math. In addition to the persistence I began learning in middle school, graduate studies revealed that solving a new problem requires ingenuity and creativity. Anything I naturally lacked in these categories I compensated for with stubborn optimism and reckless experimentation. What do you do if you can't tell whether your conjecture is true? Test it by trying every example you can come up with. If, after recycling reams of scratch paper and reducing pounds of chalk to dust, you think it might be true, try to prove it. If you can't prove it, try every potential candidate for a counterexample that could possibly disprove it. This "try anything and every-

> **Insight comes to those who experiment, fail, and try, try again (*ad nauseum*)... and, above all, if you persist in math you can learn to persist in all things.**

thing" strategy was ultimately what landed results for me, and I discovered that my success depended on a great deal of work that was wrong or seemed to lead nowhere.

This exercise in relentless persistence actually honed my intuition. More significantly, the steely focus I developed in the process continues to transcend subject matter. In the ninety-first mile of a recent century ride—inching uphill, in the heat, with legs of spaghetti—the resolve to continue came from the same place it did in those years of training to become a mathematician. I didn't know if I could finish, but I had developed the capacity to keep trying. (It worked. I made it.)

So, what do I do for a living? I teach math! But what do I really do? I try to pass on the things that math has taught me over the years: Insight comes to those who experiment, fail, and try, try again (*ad nauseum*); mathematical thinking provides powerful ways of considering and understanding the world; and, above all, if you persist in math you can learn to persist in all things.

1. The proof invokes the Mean Value Theorem, which implies that at some moment in time Ed must have been driving *exactly* 73.2 mph, the average speed for the trip.

2. This is indeed the real name.

The Brightening of Stars

Alexandra Merley Hill

German Professor Alexandra Merley Hill specializes in contemporary German literature and culture and in women's writing in German. She is co-editor of the books *Germany in the Loud Twentieth Century* and *German Women's Writing in the Twenty-First Century*, and author of *Playing House: Motherhood, Intimacy, and Domestic Spaces in Julia Franck's Fiction*.

How vividly I remember sitting in my college advisor's office during the fall of my senior year. It seems that it was always cold outside, and I could feel the cold seeping through the floor-length windows of the 1950s concrete building. Yet the atmosphere in my advisor's office was lamp-lit, warm, and giving off the heat of my (bruised) ego. I was applying for a Fulbright English Teaching Assistantship to Germany, and my German advisor was reading, re-reading, critiquing, chopping up, and discarding significant portions of my application essays. Although I attended one of the Seven Sister Schools, with a reputation for academic excellence, no professor had ever been so hard on my work before. A straight-A student who, until college, had been able to skate along relatively unchallenged, I was drawn to a group of faculty (in the German Department) who saw that I was capable of more and pushed me hard to reach for it. Never as a freshman would it have occurred to me to apply for a prestigious Fulbright fellowship, but my professors saw something in me that I hadn't seen in myself. This path was much more challenging than the one I had trodden in high school. At the end of one of these essay-reading appointments, tired of grappling with each word, emotionally entangled in what I was writing, and chagrined at the number of typos found in my essays, I just barely made it out the office door before bursting into tears. My very kind and patient advisor welcomed me back the next time with no reference to my emotional outburst and struck that delicate balance between making me feel both welcome and uncomfortable. For no growth comes from a state of comfort. Quite the opposite, I believe. We must be uncomfortable to grow our intellects, our philosophies, our relationships, and our hearts. To paraphrase a colleague, college students shouldn't be bored and at ease. If they are, they are not growing.

Looking back, how I came to study German can be considered coincidental—or perhaps providential—but it was only tangential. It is not really about Goethe, the Berlin Wall, or East German film. At several junctures in my education I continued with German simply because of the people: my college professor who insisted I take one more German class when I wanted to quit; the advisor who made me rewrite application essays until I cried; my *Doktormutter* (doctor "mother") who contested my inclination to wrap up stories with neat bows; my best friend from graduate school with whose brilliance I still scramble to keep up; my feminist colleagues in the profession who campaign for higher adjunct wages and better systems of mentoring; and my beloved colleagues at the university who believe we can always do better by our students. Not so much seeking out German itself, I sought out people who challenged me, who pushed me—and continue to push me—to grow, stretch, bend, and change.

Now a professor in my own right, I see it as my challenge to help students grow, stretch, bend, and change. I do that by pushing them to read, write, and speak more and more German; to live in and deeply understand cultures beyond the familiar; to seek out and engage with things that inspire them; to dream up futures well beyond their modest freshman-year plans. I love interesting students. I love the ones who surprise me with their creative ideas and great insights. I love the ones who make me laugh and who connect genuinely and open-heartedly with people. I love the ones who are earnest about exploring the world, who are dedicated

> I sought out people who challenged me, who pushed me— and continue to push me—to grow, stretch, bend, and change.

to learning despite and because of their realization that they know so little. I love the ones who are committed to their growth as humans and caring members of our campus community. But this is not who students are yet when they arrive at college or university—they don't arrive fully formed. What would be the fun in that? A particular joy and privilege of teaching in higher education is watching students grow from freshman to senior year and beyond and actively fostering that growth. My work is about supporting them and cheering them on, while pushing them beyond the limit of what they think they can do.

How I engage with students and what happens between us changes with each year of their progress. In the classroom, I maintain a tricky balance between creating a safe space for students to be comfortable with themselves and uncomfortable with hard material. But half of our relationship develops outside the classroom as we reflect together on what they learned about the language, the culture, and themselves while studying abroad, interning at the German American School of Portland, or bringing the fields of German Studies and Social Work in dialogue. We also commit to the inten-

tional process of braiding together different ribbons of interest (English literature, gender studies, and German; or German, business, and travel) and figuring out how the strands come together. Finally, we plan: mining wells of interest for senior-year theses or conference papers and working on applications for the Fulbright ETA program (an opportunity for both the student and myself to reflect on who we are and the paths we have taken).

And what my students—our students—accomplish is amazing. One young man, with a genius for languages, studied German and Spanish at the Univeristy of Portland, studied in Austria and Spain, taught himself Portuguese and some Turkish, and then spent a year volunteering at an orphanage in Honduras as part of the Jesuit Volunteer Corps. One young woman fed her voracious appetite for learning by majoring in German and Sociology, with an informal focus on migrants' and women's issues. After spending a year in Germany on a Fulbright grant, she joined Teach for America and now serves underprivileged youth in a public elementary school in Tennessee. Two recent graduates are best friends teaching English in Hamburg this year. Their varied paths and interests (a dancer interested in museum work, a skateboarder working with ESL students) bring them to the same point at the same time. German has, fortuitously, brought all these bright stars across my path.

The list of stories goes on, and I think fondly of each of these students, taking special delight in seeing how they have pushed *themselves*. I can't hide how hard this process is; it's common for frustration to drive students to tears. (Having learned from my own experience, I have tissues and chocolate on my desk for them at all times.) I should confess that pushing my students is not easy for me, either. Exhausting, emotionally draining—these are two phrases that come immediately to mind. It's horrible to make students cry! But what kind of teacher would I be if I didn't push *myself*? We all emerge stronger for it.

So what does what I *really* teach students have to do with German? Honestly, not a whole lot. German may be the subject that I teach, but "teaching German" is really the name of the road on which I travel in the uphill, often surprising, and occasionally truly stellar paths of the intellectual and personal growth of my students.

Opening the Door

Matthew Warshawsky

International Languages and Cultures Professor Matthew Warshawsky is a scholar of early modern Spain as well as of Jewish cultural and literary expression in the Iberian world. His publications have appeared in books and journals focusing on Hispanic and Jewish topics, and he was the recipient of the University of Portland's award for outstanding scholarship in 2014.

Studying a language opens the door to a lot more than nouns and verbs. It creates a space in which students and professors can learn lessons for navigating life itself and gain skills in cross-cultural interpersonal communication focused on respect. As a professor of Spanish, I may never have come to this realization had it not been for the passion of my own Spanish professors. Their enthusiasm for this language and Spanish-speaking cultures was so infectious that I wanted to emulate them, be them, and even imitate their speech outside of class. Sometimes I would find myself walking across the campus green, repeating whole phrases they had just enunciated in lectures and discussions. Their own rich vocabulary planted the seed for the growth of my own linguistic passion. Studying abroad in Spain during part of my junior year in college cemented my drive to learn more. I relished the serendipity with which everything I was learning seemed to coalesce, such that images from Francisco de Goya's dark and satirical paintings at the Prado Museum were referenced next in a novel I was reading for a contemporary narrative class. I drank in all of these experiences, delved into the links between them, and discovered a thriving Spanish connection in everything I was experiencing. I knew then that I wanted to be a professor of Spanish.

As educators and mentors, we have the profound opportunity to influence students during a time of potentially great transformation in their own lives by asking, and then helping them answer, important questions. For example, what are the lessons learned from studying other cultures? How can learning the sounds and stories of a new language and culture, both written and visual, inform our understanding of the world in which we live? A starting point in our educational journey is respect for the importance of structure. Just as scientific formulas help explain how the natural world functions and understanding the rules of the road enables us to drive safely, the rules of grammatical precision help us create and convey meaning from person to person. Recognizing patterns of verb endings, placement of accents in writing and speech, and agreement of gender and number in the use of nouns and adjectives emphasizes the importance of attention to detail and the consequences of small errors, just as a small error in a scientific calculation can lead to an inaccurate conclusion. For example, no one wishing to describe the symmetry of a *panal,* or honeycomb, and the buzzing about of bees there, would want to confuse this word with *pañal,* or diaper. Thus, by correcting and expanding their own written and spoken Spanish, students learn to communicate their ideas in ways that are clear and grammatically accurate, which is a critical life lesson.

As a corollary and contrast to the first lesson, a second lesson is the recognition that we can strive for excellence by expressing ourselves in a language other than our first despite making mistakes doing so. Students of a new language shouldn't silence their voices for fear of inaccuracy, particularly when communicating ideas in front of peers. Envisioning the study of Spanish as a journey rather than a destination centers the experience on learning itself. Instead of trying to achieve linguistic perfection, we can deepen our engagement with the language knowing that errors of grammar and vocabulary are an inevitable and important part of the learning process. I encourage students to express their ideas not by translating them from English or another language to Spanish, but by thinking directly in Spanish using structures and words they already know. Just recently, for example, during a class in which we were discussing the nature of popular festivals in Mexico, a student who did not know the word for "fireworks" *(petardos)*, an important part of many such celebrations in Latin America, conveyed the meaning of this term with other words and even body language.

A third lesson is appreciating the parallels between learning a language and managing life itself: There are rules and exceptions to rules, and neither of these conditions is mutually exclusive. Studying a language helps the mind become more flexible and nimble. Students want to learn fixed rules of grammar that they can file away in their minds, but grammar, similar to life, is nuanced, complex, and reflective of the interplay of people of various backgrounds. For example, while most nouns in Spanish that end in "a" are feminine in gender, many that end in "ma" are masculine, reflecting the influence of Greek on the evolution of the language. Thus, studying grammar models the reality that life cannot be reduced to absolutes. We also see this truth in verbs with irregular endings. These exceptions to the rules contribute to the richness and depth of the language, just as historical contradictions and anomalies show that life is more complicated and antithetical than it might appear at first. Or, as I like to say to students, the grey area of what is exceptional and even ambiguous often is more interesting than that which is sure and predictable.

> **The grey area of what is exceptional and even ambiguous often is more interesting than that which is sure and predictable.**

Finally, as a teacher of medieval, Renaissance, and Baroque Spanish literature and culture, I invite students to see the past as a tool for making sense of the present. This lesson seems especially important in a society that questions the relevance of the humanities and tends to validate Spanish principally for its "practical" applications. A good place to start our backwards journey to the present is *Don Quixote,* by Miguel de Cervantes, published in two parts 400 years ago and perhaps the most well-known novel in the Spanish language. The eponymous hero is actually an ordinary country gentleman, Alonso Quijano, who reads so many novels of chivalry that he loses his mind and decides to reinvent himself in the mold of the heroes of these texts so he might help the afflicted and right all manner of wrongs. Never mind the fact that he is a gaunt, middle-aged man wearing rusted armor, riding a skinny nag, and accompanied by a simpleton for a sidekick, Sancho Panza. Don Quixote's idealism and desire to make the world a better place no matter the obstacles resonate with students today, even when they see that the hero is an anachronism who can only recover his supposedly lost reason by renouncing his dream. A course in medieval Spanish takes us back even further, to the end of the first millennium, as a way to understand the present, leading us to ask if the *convivencia*, or coexistence, that defined relations between Christians, Muslims, and Jews in Spain at that time could prevail in today's fractured world. The past matters, because it teaches us to appreciate Don Quixote's modernity and the universality of human desire to live lives that matter, and also demonstrates how believers of three great but distinct religions relied on varying degrees of collaboration with one another. Perhaps by stepping through a door to the past, students can gain important insights that equip them on the road to the future in order to better interact with cultures evolved from this past.

It Doesn't Have to *Match*, It Just Has to Go

Stephanie Salomone

Mathematics Professor Stephanie Salomone is a dedicated teacher, pure mathematician, and the recipient of the University of Portland's award for outstanding teaching in 2009. She has received several grants to support mathematics education, outreach, and recruitment of K-12 science, technology, engineering, and mathematics (STEM) teachers.

The Christmas when I was fifteen, my dad gave me a box containing fourteen pair of purple socks, all in different shades. He said that he never, ever, wanted to endure another teenage meltdown from me over not having exactly the right pair of socks to match my top. It was the early 1990s and matching socks were A Thing. I had to get it right every time or I'd (obviously) be doomed to live in an abyss of nothingness where "they" send people who cannot manage to do things The Right Way. A social outcast! A dropout of the School of Gap, where the salespeople actually asked if you wanted matching socks whenever you bought a pocket tee!

This need to do things The Right Way permeated all that I did at age fifteen. Straight-A student. Community volunteer. Daily piano practicer. I did what was expected in the way it was expected, every single time. I had creativity in spades, but when I really applied my creativity to something I did so because it would likely earn me a better grade and not because there was some innate understanding of the importance of exceeding expectations *and* expressing who I was *at the same time*. It's not totally surprising, this desire for conformity. Matching expectations served me well. I succeeded by many measures and certainly by all academic ones. The problem was that I'd never considered other ways to perform, or learn, or succeed, much less that these more creative ways had the potential to offer me more satisfaction and happiness. Additionally, it never occurred to me that matching, doing things The Right Way, might not work for everyone, or even more elusively, that there might not be a *single* right way to get things done well.

I blame knitting and teaching mathematics for my transformation from following existing rules to making my own, from doing what works for others to doing what works for me and helping others do the same. The knitting thing is easy to explain. I could only make so many scarves in shades of dun before boredom and Kaffe Fassett, renowned international textile artist, stepped in and made me see that color and pattern made *everything* more interesting, from process to product. The mathematics thing is harder to explain, but it's not so much of a stretch.

After seeing a few years of students come in and out of my college classroom, I noted trends and now work hard to get students to buck them. Students come into mathematics with a set of what we call "nonavailing beliefs." That is, they believe there is only one way to solve a math problem, a single answer, one logical argument, one stark matching of clothes without shading or variation. They are sure there will be no flashes of insight and that light and creativity play no part of the process. This is more often than not how they have been taught in the past, and this steadfast belief can be a huge barrier to success and enjoyment, to a love of learning, to understanding one's self, and to academic and personal progress.

Learning mathematics is no more "one size fits all" than fashion and sock matching is, and I mean that from the perspective of both a teacher and a learner. The onus lies on all of us in the classroom to foster an environment where students find what brings them success. For some it's listening, but for most it's doing. It's doing *incorrectly over and over and over* until the shades of correct are discovered, blended, and sometimes even created. Over

> I blame knitting and teaching mathematics for my transformation from following existing rules to making my own, from doing what works for others to doing what works for me and helping others do the same.

the years, my teaching has evolved to accommodate different ways of learning, to encourage students to leverage their strengths and then empower them to find their own ways to learn and explain and delve deeper. I show how the vagaries of the English language (e.g., that the word *base* means the bottom, except when it doesn't, that *normal* means about twenty different things in the math world, most of which have nothing to do with conforming to a standard) lead to different and equally viable mathematical arguments, ways of looking at the world, shapes of space. I ask them to consider that if our words—which I so rarely considered in my early days of matching students' expectations of a colorless math lecture—can lead to so many interpretations, then how might we form ways to judge what is right and correct and true and well-reasoned? The answer to so many mathematics questions—unsatisfactory as it may be—is "It depends." That's not loosey-goosey nonsense. There *are* right answers and wrong answers. There are rules, some strict, some bendable. The point is that success in mathematics comes in all shades of colors, and if we push students to find out what works *for them* and then say, "Now do *that*. Now do it *again*," they thrive.

Many mathematical breakthroughs came from someone, somewhere, musing, "What if...?" Throwing caution to the wind and moving forward with confidence and the knowledge that the potential for a catastrophic outcome is rare, but students can embrace this mindset once they are convinced that being wrong isn't all that bad as long as something is learned, either about the problem or about themselves as learners. They embrace originality and creative thinking once they understand that I want them to put a bit of *themselves* into their work, even if it clashes with my plan. I want to see who they are and, more importantly, I want them to see who they might become. I want to see how I can help them get from here to there.

In the end, some of my students find that what worked for my prescriptive fifteen-year-old self works for them as well. Some veer off course slightly and break a few rules here and there. Others though, and these are the ones who truly inspire me, come into class thinking that "this math thing" isn't for them because they don't fit the mold they believe exists. They then discover that there *is* room for their purple shirt and yellow socks after all! They may not *match*, but they *go*. And they keep *going*.

Halfway Between the Head and the Heart

Nicole Leupp Hanig

Music Professor Nicole Leupp Hanig is the director of the Vocal Studies Program at the University of Portland. She's appeared as a soloist throughout the United States, Europe, and Asia, most notably with the Maggio Musicale Festival in Italy and the Pacific Music Festival in Japan.

I am a voice teacher. I teach my students classical vocal technique, repertoire, and performance, which allows them to create compelling performances of music written largely between 1600 and now, in a variety of languages, in a concert hall, over an orchestra, without a microphone.

I am passionate about vocal music. The voice is the instrument that all humans possess. Learning how to extend the use of one's voice and to conceive of the voice as an instrument is transformative for students at any level. Neurologists teach us that singing triggers more brain function at once than any other activity. In vocal study, we learn about our anatomy and physiology that allows us to sing, the acoustical properties of sound, and how we create vocal resonance. We discover the way composers set words to music to illuminate their meaning and how we, as singers, can assist in this illumination when we synthesize artistry, science, and athleticism through singing. One of my teachers used to remind me that, "The larynx sits halfway between the head and the heart." This exquisitely simple observation is always with me when I teach. We use our minds and bodies to increase our manipulation of vocal resonance, range, breath control, and stamina. We strive to understand the meaning and pronunciation of texts in our own language and others. But ultimately our goal is one of the heart— to use our voices to show something of ourselves and to do it with enough thought, power, and sincerity that we honor the composer while inspiring thought, emotion, and—if we are lucky—transcendence in the listener.

Music and singing have been a constant in my life. My parents grew up in the Mennonite church where music came only from the human voice—an instrument fashioned by God, rather than a piano or organ, in which God had no direct hand. Although my exposure to the Mennonite services was sporadic due to my parent's decision to leave the rigidity of the Mennonites for the Presbyterians, we still upheld the tradition of strong hymn singing in four-part harmony. I sat between the bass-baritone of my father and my mother, who traded alto and soprano duties with me throughout the services. The three of us sang at home, at church, and on long car trips. Vocal music was the backdrop against which I grew up, never considering that I would devote my life to this art form. I read voraciously, pursued many activities, grew curious about the wider world, and started taking language classes. I was a foreign exchange student in high school. When I went to college, I went to a school with strong language programs and planned to get a liberal arts degree that would prepare me for the Foreign Ser-

vice Exam. Cleverly, I made sure that this school also had a great choir!

I chose the Lutherans to assist me in my quest for a college education that included choral singing and attended Concordia College in Moorhead, Minnesota, home of the Concordia Choir conducted by Rene Clausen, which is one of the best college choirs in the nation. I had a successful audition and began taking voice lessons, as this was required of all its members. Voice lessons introduced me to the connection between artistry and athleticism that defines classical singing technique. Not only could I blend my voice with others to make music as part of an ensemble, I could cultivate in my own voice the strength and unique tone needed to be heard as a soloist over an ensemble. By my junior year, my voice teacher gave me the standard speech one gives to young musicians. "If you think that you can be satisfied performing in community choirs and amateur shows while pursuing another career, then you should. If you feel that you won't be satisfied unless you push yourself to your full potential as a singer and musician and aspire to making music at a professional level, you should major in music and look toward operatic study at the graduate level." I realized that all of my study in the areas of history, language, literature, and theology combined beautifully with my musical studies to prepare me for graduate study. None of the time spent outside my newly found area of specialization was wasted. Vocal music synthesized it all.

So, what do I *really* teach? What I *really* teach Is as varied as my own education and experience, which has made me the musician I am today. I teach students to enjoy making sound, to love language, to use music as a lens through which they can view culture, history, science, philosophy, theology, and more. I teach students to love music enough to explore and dissect the profound way music connects and affects all of humanity and also to be awed and humbled by its mystery. We know that musical training encourages problem solving, discipline, effective communication, and cultivates connectivity between right-brain and left-brain thinking. I strive to teach all of these things by having high expectations of my students and, more importantly, encouraging them to have

> I teach students to love music enough to explore and dissect the profound way music connects and affects all of humanity and also to be awed and humbled by its mystery.

high expectations of themselves. My aim is to inspire students to learn without placing limits on themselves: to challenge students to think beyond what they perceive of as their capabilities.

The study of vocal music teaches students to perceive of themselves in a new way. Social Psychologist Amy Cuddy of Harvard University has shown in her research that a powerful stance changes not only others' perceptions of us but more importantly it changes our perception of ourselves. I observe this change every day as timid performers learn to maintain the bodily alignment and stance needed for efficient/powerful singing and challenge themselves to convey confidence on stage through their fear. As their technique strengthens, their confidence and composure grow, both onstage and off.

Many people think that the ability to sing is a gift, and they are right. It is a gift that every person on earth has a powerful musical instrument resting beneath their chin that can both create a melodic sound and use that melodic sound to even greater purpose: to transport language, prose, and poetry. There is no magic wand waved, however, when we learn to use our bodies and minds to create these things. The ability to sing is not given, but earned. It requires diligence, discipline, and practice. In the end, I hope I teach what all great teachers do: that we are never finished and that joy in life comes from knowing that the work is never done. The acquisition of skill and knowledge is not a means to an end. Rather it is both the means and the end.

Part IV

Engage

"Whatever you are, be a good one."—Abraham Lincoln

Prologue

Shannon Mayer

At the end of the day, the question remains, "Does all this education matter?" Do the skills and experiences, the moments of self-discovery and authentic connection students experience at college or university impact them in a way that makes them *awake* and changes how they ultimately live their lives and engage the world? We college and university teachers believe the answer is a resounding yes. The professor-authors of these final essays explore ways in which education can impact a student's *way of being* in the world.

The Urgency of Slowness

Lars Larson

English Professor Lars Erik Larson's research explores the representation and circulation of material spaces, including systems of infrastructure, cities, and regions. He is the recipient of the University of Portland's award for outstanding teaching in 2013 and a Fulbright grant to Mysore, India, to teach about spatial approaches to literature. He's directed the University of Portland's Writing Program and published essays on Bollywood road films, the American interstate system in Kerouac's *On the Road*, and an overview of road-book scholarship. He has given papers on mobility in Cheryl Strayed's *Wild*, abandoned landscapes in Western literature, and John McPhee's study of deep time in American geology.

"Hey man slow down."—Radiohead, O.K. Computer

In my neighborhood, someone's posted an official-looking sign to an audience of automotive readers: "Drive Like Your Kids Live Here." As with most literary texts, this work of roadside micro-literature invites readers to a game of imagination. Its author asks us to enact a fiction, to project ourselves into the mindset of the nervous resident parents. Doing so, we might voluntarily change our perspective. We'll switch the moment's priorities from casual haste and efficiency to safety, all in the name of empathy, understanding, and life itself.

Speed is one of the grand pleasures of modernity. I love the sensation as much as anyone: the frictionless freeway, Google's instant answers, email's immediacy. Streaming, surfing, scrolling. Hurtling 500 miles per hour through cloud landscapes while noshing peanuts.

But as the sign on the road reminds us, there are places in this world for re-learning the urgency of slowness. A literature class is one of them.

Technology has trained several generations of eyes to read screens in jerky saccades. But college re-trains us to read with what our English Department's former leader Herman Asarnow calls "slow eyes." As it takes time to process the complexities of the world, a literature ambitious enough to represent those complexities will demand special skills: impulse control, patience, attention. Pico Iyer observes in his book *The Art of Stillness* that technology has given us a new need: "The ability to gather information, which used to be so crucial, is now far less important than the ability to sift through it."

Pensive encounters with stories are one mode of sifting. In reading with a speed limit, we make time to sort and reflect on the world. Time to learn the names of our troubles, and those of others. Time to recognize our better selves in storied examples. By slowing down, we notice wordsmiths who bend old language in new ways. Who bust through our shopworn realities to equip us with the tools of new perspectives. Whose verbal ballistics arrow deep into our brains, lodging for decades.

Like no other language, poetry rewards the slowest eye. The more carefully we read, the more miraculously poetry speaks. The speaker in Wislawa Szymborska's "Miracle Fair" points out in astonishment that "the unthinkable / can be thought." But this only happens when we draw as much upon our imagination as we do our brightly-lit technologies.

Reading drama—the blueprint for a play, written not for the eye but for a director to translate into bodies, voices, and stagecraft—has its own rewards. With slow eyes, the reader takes a subversive peek behind the curtain at a playwright's plan, and does all casting, staging, and directing in the mind's theater. Here, we confront life's heart-ache, and the thousand natural shocks that we—as Hamlet noticed one dark day—are heir to. We come to recognize that the things of this world have a plot—including the arc of our lives. Our awareness of this cause-and-effect structure may be the difference between whether we choose the plot for our life, or someone else does.

But so often our imaginations fail us. When our curiosity narrows to a pinhole, the fictions of others restore our sense of life's options. And fiction at its best offers an inkling of life's immensity. Characters invite us to see and poke and prod the ambient social values around us, rather than to adopt them unthinkingly. Symbolism, slowly turned over in the mind, makes us aware of the implications that arise from such things as a war, a whale, a proposal, or a glance. The patient fiction reader learns the pleasures of inter-textuality—when stories reference, rewrite, or remix previous stories. In these and other ways, fiction enlarges our imaginations and ourselves. That's why our city's engine of literary promotion—Portland Literary Arts—defines literature as "an *immersive* art form. The degree to which the reader plays an essential creative role makes literature distinctive from all other art forms."

A teacher's creative role in exploring a semester's bundle of stories requires the skill of listening. In this era, when you can't swing a selfie-stick without hitting a student busy texting-while-learning, that means having students do less rather than more. Not less work, but uni-tasking our main goal: sharpening our receptiveness to achieve the rewards of slowness. As Matthew Crawford reminds us in his study of the fruits of attention *(The World Beyond Your Head: On Becoming an Individual in an Age of Distraction),* "one consumes a great deal of silence in the course of becoming educated."

But the social nature of knowledge means we cannot learn alone, always in silence. We have to bump up against each other in order to *know* better. The simple classroom remains a brilliant technology invented for this purpose. Sudden outbreaks of intelligence arise most often from individual, small-group, or whole-class airings of possible interpretations, whether of the cartoon realities of Alison Bechdel's *Fun Home,* the phantasmagoric experiences of Ralph Ellison's *Invisible Man,* or the refusals of Herman Melville's *Bartleby.* My role is not to teach an etiquette of appreciation, for like so many disciplines, English has moved away from teaching merely the "What" of a fixed body of knowledge in favor of pursuing the "How" and the "Why" of things. By marinating in literature's worlds, we practice collaboratively confronting the world and its ways.

Columbia English professor Andrew Delbanco insists that college is not for getting what you want; it's for figuring out what's worth having. A life-enhancing slowness aids this figuring. I know the habit doesn't make for a compelling university motto ("The University of Portland: Crawl!"). And it won't aid every discipline or task (Track & Field?).

But literature—whether in the form of a novel, a song, or a street sign—points us to places with a salient

> **Sudden outbreaks of intelligence arise most often from individual, small-group, or whole-class airings of possible interpretations.**

need for slowness. Here in "the darkness, in this twittering world," we try not to end up with the bleak regret of T.S. Eliot's speaker in *Four Quartets:* "We had the experience but missed the meaning." The slow habits of a literature class—or a life finely observed—habituate us to a lifetime of marrying experience with meaning.

Engineering Creativity

Heather Dillon

Mechanical Engineering Professor Heather Dillon specializes in renewable energy, energy efficiency, and heat transfer applications. She is the author of numerous journal articles. Examples of her mathematics and engineering-inspired photography can be found at: http://www.heatherdillon.com/Math/Math/

Imagine the most stereotypical engineering students possible. (You might picture pocket protectors, green graph paper, and large calculators at the ready.) They studiously peer up from a dense stack of books and smile as they derive immense joy from a complex mathematical derivation.

Now, consider the smart phone, the St. John's Bridge, a wind turbine. These are just a few examples of engineering innovations that are beautifully complex and intricately beautiful. How do you engineer creativity? How do you foster innovative thinking?

As a child I never imagined I would become an engineer. I was not particularly good at math or science, but instead thrived on art. I knew my color wheel before I could read and could mix oil paints like an old master before I finished fourth grade. Every teacher applauded my efforts at sculpture and ink sketching but fell silent on my practice of long division. While visiting prospective colleges an architecture professor suggested that I was more likely to be admitted to the program if I started as an engineering major and completed the required mathematics courses before I applied to the program. It was a slight misdirection that led me to a startlingly creative career in engineering.

Now as I teach mechanical engineering courses at the university level, I try to help my students appreciate the importance creativity will play in their potential engineering careers. Creativity and innovation have propelled our technology to amazing new frontiers. The design of the iPhone represented the creative genius of Steve Jobs and the team of engineers that managed to build the revolutionary device.

The idea of integrating science and art has existed for hundreds of years, and in fact a division between humanities and science has only emerged in modern times. Great historical scientists like Leonardo DaVinci were also known for artistic skill. As we contemplate massive engineering challenges like climate change, information security, bio-engineering, and space exploration only the most creative solutions will help society leap successfully to the next era.

I use art in my courses to help students explore creativity. My students are often shocked to enter a rigorous class on thermodynamics (energy systems) and find that one of the requirements for the course is an original art project. Thermodynamics is a difficult course for many undergraduate students due to the intricate mathematics and the complex nature of the concepts learned, so I challenge them to represent a physical principle studied in class using an art medium of their choice (music, poetry, essay, painting). They have explored complex topics like enthalpy (energy flowing in a system), entropy (a match burning, unable to return to its pre-ignited state), and exergy (the maximum possible energy that could be used in a system). To lead them into their own artistic exploration I show them artistic interpretations of each concept from prior student work. I also share my own artistic work exploring mathematics through photography and bring to class humorous cartoons that illustrate the irony of energy conservation.

I have seen a different type of engineering student emerge as they immerse themselves in the thermodynamics of creativity. Suddenly *the same students* are wearing a rainbow of acrylic paint and chatting about the merits of iambic pentameter in the context of entropy. They are speckled in unintentional glitter, chipping away at a wax sculpture, and reshaping expectations of their

> I have seen a different type of engineering student emerge as they immerse themselves in the thermodynamics of creativity.

own futures. There are few sights as beautiful as watching deeply analytical engineering students fully immerse themselves in art.

There are always a few reluctant students who are hesitant to try this. They claim they are not good at "art" and wish for nothing more than the familiar comfort of a challenging calculation. I suspect there is more at work here than a desire for the familiar. Creativity requires a certain type of bravery, a willingness to reveal a deeper part of one's self than is called out in the solving of a complex equation. To ease the transition for these reluctant adventurers, I point out that a Haiku requires strong counting skills and reassure them that projects will be graded on scientific merit rather than artistic merit. In the end, they all choose to use a creative medium rather than perform an extra mathematical derivation to complete the assignment.

Through the creative process my students become free from the predictable safety of calculations and instead create objects that speak clearly to the world about the innovation of engineers. They learn to express themselves to people outside the engineering field with amazing confidence and poise. They become inspired by the beauty of the science rather than hindered by the complexity of the calculations. They find joy in engineering and in creativity. They reshape their expectations—about themselves and about engineering.

As I reflect on my own engineering career, I sometimes wonder what type of artist I might have become. I believe I would have specialized in sculpture, the type of sculpture where the artist visualizes the outline of a person and slowly molds the vision from metal or clay. As an engineering professor I now sculpt every day, but the medium has changed. I invite students to integrate creativity and thermodynamics so they can create innovative devices and solve complex problems. I teach thermodynamics, but I also teach creativity.

Wide Awake

Rich Christen

Education Professor Rich Christen studies the historical, social, and cultural foundations of current schooling and other educational practices. He has published his work in history, American studies, and history-of-education journals, has contributed to articles in *The New York Times*, *The Boston Globe*, and *The Oregonian*, and has received research grants from the Spencer Foundation and the Newberry Library.

"Not everything that can be counted counts, and not everything that counts can be counted."[1]
—William Bruce Cameron

Primary and secondary education and the education of primary and secondary teachers is rapidly becoming what Peter Taubman and others refer to as an "audit culture." Standards written by policymakers, professional organizations, and business entities now describe in minute detail what every child needs to know to function effectively in the global economy of the twenty-first century…and what every teacher should do to guarantee that the prescribed knowledge is learned. Government, parents, the media, accreditors, and countless other "auditors" demand evidence that the standards have been taught and learned, generating batteries of tests and other assessments as well as an endless stream of data—most of it numerical—to rate the quality of students, teachers, and schools.

It is difficult to argue with some aspects of this model. There are important skills that students should learn in every subject. Who would disagree with the Common Core State Standards insistence that sixth grade students should learn to "explain how an author develops the point of view of the narrator or speaker in a text," for example? It is also undoubtedly important to know if instruction is working, especially for groups schools have persistently underserved over the years.

Still, as a teacher educator with over forty years of experience in the classroom, I can't shake the feeling that something is wrong with the audit culture. My stomach churns as I sit through seemingly endless meetings discussing the importance of standards, assessments, rubrics, and data. I toss and turn at night, disturbed by increasing demands to distill my courses to a set of standards and aligned assessments. I am repelled rather than reassured by the standard setters' claims that we can codify what every child needs and the test makers' dictum that everything that counts can be counted. Such assertions ignore our increasingly fluid and diverse world and stifle the creativity required for innovation, encouraging factory-like schools where, as observed by early twentieth-century educator Ellwood Cubberley, children are "shaped and formed into finished products…manufactured like nails." They reduce learning to a pre-determined list of knowledge and skills, flouting the individuality of students and buttressing the interests of the privileged. Most ominously, they embody hubris: a self-destructive arrogance that regulates the voices of students, stifles the search for new ideas, and discourages alternative ways of doing things.

I do my best teaching when I encourage students to look at familiar things in new ways and to explore and express new possibilities—to become, in the words of philosopher of education Maxine Greene, "wide awake." In my education courses, for example, I use readings, field experiences, discussions, and other activities to create spaces where students can critically examine how schools currently work in American society. Over time, they begin to see that students do not experience American schools in the same ways, that schools privilege some while marginalizing others. This awareness spurs them to consider the possibility that things should and can be different and to collectively explore what these differences might look like. Over the years, I have learned that "wide awakeness"—for both students and myself—best happens when I resist the temptation to shape students in my own image or standards, when I allow students to debate, process, and discover in a community that I am a part of but do not control, and when I treat unexpected ideas and unintended learning as joyous discoveries rather than unproductive deviations.

One joyous discovery occurred in a recent class discussion when a student proposed that thinking of education as a love story rather than as a research project collecting data on students would open up new possibilities for learning. I was intrigued by this thought, and decided to explore it in class, even though it meant putting aside the day's plans. Some students embraced the love-story metaphor and its implications that education is more about mutual relationships, caring, acceptance, and growth than about competition and achievement. Others found the metaphor too soft. Successful learning, they argued, was more about hard work, perseverance, struggle, and even boredom than about the feel-good aspects of a love story. Eventually, a student posited the concept of marriage as a way to connect the two. Marriages, she argued, involve both: hard work, monotony, and conflict balanced with and even fueled by a profound connection to another and meaningful growth as individuals and as a couple. As a result of this discussion, the class—both the students and I—deepened our understanding of what the educational process can do for individuals and communities. We were awakened to new possibilities, developing, in Greene's words, "the sense of agency required for living a moral life."

> True dialogue is a mutual, non-hierarchical encounter, a way of learning and knowing about others where each individual possesses equal agency and voice.

Dialogue between teacher and student is a pre-condition for wide awakeness, according to philosopher Paolo Freire. But true dialogue, Freire insists, is more than simple communication between two individuals. It is a mutual, non-hierarchical encounter, a way of learning and knowing about others where each individual possesses equal agency and voice. As a teacher, I aim to facilitate Freirian classroom dialogues, conversations where students and I are co-investigators, both eager to learn about each other and the world, both open to the possibility of new knowledge and change. Aware that dialogue is damaged when the teacher sets herself or himself apart as the sole owner and communicator of truth, I avoid whenever possible the role of all-knowing director and interrogator. Instead, I try to present my knowledge and perspectives for the students' consideration while encouraging them to form and express their own opinions.

I also make sure that students are not the only ones to share experiences, answer questions, reconsider positions, and take risks. I invite students to critique my perspectives just as I do theirs, and when I ask students to discuss their own experiences I make sure that I share my own, both successes and failures. I also frequently give students an opportunity to comment on the readings, activities, and processes we use in class, encouraging them to give me feedback and to consider how what we do in class might be used in their future classrooms. Observations range from feel-good praise to biting critique. Some students have challenged certain readings as racist; others have pointed out gender bias in the ways I operate the classroom. Such comments are not easy to hear, especially in a classroom setting. But they work to create an authentic conversation with the goals of improvement and wide awakeness for me as well as the students.

Freirian dialogue and the wide awakeness it engenders are lofty and challenging educational goals.

They ask me to reject the common notion of teacher as the sole expert in the classroom and to become vulnerable, to publicly open myself to the growth and transformation that are usually reserved for students. The audit culture's model of education—what Freire dismissively refers to as "banking education"—can be especially alluring to standards-equipped educators who have reduced the educational process to a simple formula: identify what students need to know and do; design and execute instruction that inculcates the desired knowledge and skills; then implement assessments to determine whether or not the learning has happened.

But meaningful education, I have come to realize over the course of my career, is more complex. It requires teachers as well as students to throw off sleep—to accept that they don't know everything, that they can't map out all that is important for students to learn, that they can't predict, quantify, or measure all valuable learning, and that education is best when it is a community-directed project, wide-awake to new ideas and possibilities.

1. William Bruce Cameron. *Informal Sociology: A Casual Introduction to Sociological Thinking* (New York: Random House, 1963).

Seeing Clearly: Lessons from Social Science and Simon the Chipmunk

Andrew Guest

Psychology and Sociology Professor Andrew Guest examines social development in cultural and community contexts. His specific points of focus include youth development in socially marginalized communities and sport-and-extracurricular programs as developmental and self-concept influences. His work is published in leading psychology and sociology journals and his most recent research looks at topics including positive youth development in high school extracurricular programs and the teaching of diversity in psychology courses.

At the end of a particularly busy recent semester, after reading through a set of student course evaluations with a few more stingers than usual, I snuck away for an afternoon children's matinee with my four-year-old son. A 2007 vintage Alvin and the Chipmunks movie was playing and, while the squealing songs didn't do much to soothe my jangled nerves, my son's laughter was a useful salve. The movie as a whole was unremarkable. The Chipmunks are displaced from the forest to the city where they discover a skill for singing, leading to clichéd life lessons about the pitfalls of fame and the value of friendship. But there was one bit that kept popping into my mind after the credits rolled. Early in the movie amidst a bit of raucous play, Simon, who had never been able to see things as clearly as his chipmunk brethren, stumbled into a pair of toy glasses that fell off a Santa doll. Suddenly, after a lifetime of blurry vision, the specs spill onto the bridge of his nose and the lenses bring the whole world into a new, clear focus.

When I think about the question of what I really teach, despite the academic temptation to cite the types of erudite scholarly work I foist upon my students, I can't get that fictional chipmunk's moment of clarity off my mind: I want to offer my students new lenses. I invite them to use the knowledge and methods they gain from social science to look at the world in unfamiliar ways, to see new questions about how society works, and to envision innovative ways of making meaning out of human experience. I really love teaching when I get to join students in doing that looking.

This love may well have started as personal need. The most significant experience of my own young adulthood was two-plus years as a Peace Corps volunteer in Malawi, a small country in southern Africa that often serves as a poster child for the demographic problems of the developing world—poverty, HIV, deforestation, etc. But in my experience working in youth development there, I found people and communities much more complex and robust than the dire statistical indicators had led me to believe. Children in Malawi often had the freedom to play and interact in ways that were at critical risk in American suburban communities. Malawian neighbors often had the deep social bonds we romanticize when discussing the ills of our urban centers. Of course, profound global inequalities also meant few of the Malawians I worked with would have the opportunities of many American children, and that tension—between human adaptation and structural deprivation—perplexed me. I came home from Malawi and found a graduate program that would allow me to develop a mix of social science lenses to help me—and, I hoped, my future students—better understand the complexities of a global society.

Now, although I'm officially an Associate Professor of Psychology, by courtesy of my colleagues and by disposition of my mind I often get to cross-list my classes in sociology with courses in the social justice program. I also regularly bring into my teaching some of my background in cultural anthropology and sport studies. So when I teach cross-listed classes such as "Children, Youth, and Society" or "Psychosocial Aspects of Sport and Physical Activity" I start the semester by asking students to think about what differ-

> I invite my students to use the knowledge and methods they gain from social science to look at the world in unfamiliar ways, to see new questions about how society works, and to envision innovative ways of making meaning out of human experience.

ent lenses might offer the subject. And then I try to offer them tools, such as ethnography, to employ those lenses through the course of the semester. Ethnography is the social science method of systematically interpreting cultural ways of life through participant-observation. It is, as goes the axiom in cultural anthropology, the process of "making the strange familiar, and the familiar strange." So, for example, when I accompanied a group of students to Cape Town, South Africa, the students spent time taking ethnographic field notes while working with youth-serving programs and regularly observed how much more prominent sibling care was in South Africa than in their own communities. We then used interviews to explore the perceived value of sibling care—the strange was becoming familiar. Which eventually led the students to also ask why sibling care is so rare in contemporary middle-class American homes—the familiar was becoming strange. At the end of the course, the students were using the language of ethnography to describe their own experience in the program. The right lenses had dropped onto their nose and over their eyes.

Teaching by offering new lenses, unfortunately, isn't always such a smooth process. One thing those recent end-of-semester student evaluations made clear was that my effort to offer new lenses in my sport class hadn't been universally popular. Students tend to take a class about sport and physical activity because they love sport and physical activity. I do too. But part of using new lenses to think about the social world is raising challenging questions and sharpening those famous "critical thinking" skills. This often means obliging students to reflect upon and reconsider deeply socialized commitments – is the sport ethic of sacrificing to go faster, higher, and stronger part of what explains cheating in sport? Is it possible that the benefits of sports are less about individual character and more about community? Is the immense commitment of time and money devoted towards an American college sports system that is unique in the world a reflection of distorted educational values? Some students get frustrated with me for raising these questions, sometimes even a bit angry, but they also admit that the questions force them to think about sport—and their own experiences and commitments—in new ways. Adjusting to new lenses isn't always easy.

Even beyond interdisciplinary courses, I love teaching our introductory General Psychology course because of the opportunity to offer students particularly psychological lenses on the world—to think systematically, empirically, scientifically, and critically about important aspects of human experience. We talk about the popularity of brightly-colored brain scans to explain everything from autism to political preferences, and then talk about why pictures of brain scans are often compelling because of mistaken assumptions about causality: brain activity is always both a cause and effect of our experiences. We talk about the various common ways people make bad decisions and then talk about why those bad decisions often highlight the efficiencies of human cognition: the mind is magnificently designed to take short-cuts. We talk about the ways that drug treatments do and do not help with psychological disorders such as depression and anxiety, and then talk about why our mental health is always a dynamic process: our psychological well-being depends on an intricate dance between biological, psychological, and social phenomena. Psychology offers lenses, if not lessons, for all of that and more.

In the latter half of that not-particularly-compelling-to-the-adult-viewer Alvin and the Chipmunks movie, when the Chipmunks have become global music celebrities, their slick manager convinces Simon his regular Santa glasses just aren't cool looking—so Simon switches to a more hip pair. But the cool new glasses don't actually help him see; they don't have the right lenses. So in a dramatic pivot, as the Chipmunks musical fame starts to wear thin, Simon stands up for himself and chooses the glasses that help him to see the world more clearly. For me, after a long semester of dealing with big ideas, the simplicity of the metaphor resonated. I don't think the same could be said for my four year-old son; he was too busy giggling at the funny voices. But I hope the broader idea will someday strike him as well. We all need a variety of metaphorical lenses—ideas, methods, theories, facts, data points, and more—to navigate an increasingly complex social world. And while I don't think students really have a distinct moment in my classes when new lenses drop over their eyes, what I really try to teach my students is that social science offers lenses for making important things clear.

Why Does This Matter? [Exactly]

Molly Hiro

English Professor Molly Hiro teaches writing and literature courses in the English department, including classes that focus on race, gender, and social change. Among her publications are several teaching-related articles on topics such as the teaching of African American literature and a how-to essay on staging an undergraduate literature conference. She was awarded a Fulbright lecturing grant to South India.

In my early years as an English professor, there was one moment I always dreaded. Most of my classroom hours (then as now) were at the introductory level, in required courses populated mostly by non-majors. Inevitably—perhaps two or three weeks into the semester, when the class might be deep in a discussion of a poem—one student would lean back in his chair (or raise her hand with a suspicious look on her face) and ask: "How can we know any of this for sure?" or "What's the point of picking apart a poem so obsessively?" or "Where does any of this get us, anyway?" Cue silence among the other twenty-four students, who would now turn their attention to the professor, waking from their poetic reverie to wonder precisely the same thing.

Familiar as this moment became, it unnerved me every time. What these bold students were really asking was "Why does the study of literature matter?" And while I'd devoted my career to the discipline, the question still wasn't easy to answer. Indeed, it's a question that drove me away from academia for a few years between college and graduate school. I loved to read, and loved even more to discuss complex works of literature around a seminar table, especially if led by a passionate professor. But the young idealist in me had trouble seeing the broader value of studying books when there were so many real-world problems that needed solving. This conviction sent me into several years of volunteer and non-profit work, until I realized for myself that teaching can become a real-world intervention, too.

For those who don't gravitate toward English as I did, the question of why we should spend time studying it becomes even more persistent. Quantitative disciplines such as science and mathematics produce the comforts of empirical, objective, and measurable results, whereas literature prefers to dwell in uncertainty and nuance. Spending your college years in professional schools of nursing, business, or engineering assures that you'll most likely become a nurse, businessperson, or engineer; but the career path of a humanities major is less clearly defined (evident in hackneyed jokes such as "What question does an English major ask? Would you like fries with that?"). In the midst of tentative economic times and looming global and environmental disasters, can we afford to while away hours reflecting on some poem written 200 years ago?

These days, I've not only refined my answer to the "Why does this matter?" question, I've made it the centerpiece of my introductory English courses. That is, while I spend the bulk of my time teaching the skills of literary analysis and writing—to read incisively, pay attention to detail, pause over surprising choices of language and form, and ultimately write persuasively and clearly about these discoveries—I also provide a bookending context. Alongside the poems, novels, and drama, we read articles and essays that confront fundamental questions: What is the point of a college literature class, or of the liberal arts more broadly? Why, indeed, read? Why read analytically? What can literature do in the world? How did people think about this in the past, and how do they think about it today?

To begin to answer these questions, we read essays that examine the value of the liberal arts, especially in an increasingly secular age that considers data and empiricism as the superior source of knowledge. Most of those jokes about English majors turn out to be untrue (for example, today's employers in all kinds of fields are seeking "soft skills" of thinking and communicating more than "hard skills" of a particular discipline; humanities majors outscore others on graduate school entrance exams). And in fact, the study of the liberal arts might even upend the presumptions upon which they are based. If (as we seem to hear all the time) the financial return on a degree in English is less than on one in engineering or economics, critic William Deresiewicz argues, that may reveal *choice* more than *necessity*: "Part of what you learn from majoring in something that actually interests you is that there are more fulfilling ways to spend your time than trying to be rich." The liberal arts may not have a self-evident practical utility, but that doesn't mean they are simply decorative; instead, says Deresiewicz, the ultimate purpose of a liberal arts education "is to help you learn to reflect in the widest and deepest sense, beyond the requirements of work and career."

So we encounter arguments about the place of the liberal arts in today's world, but we also read about the function of literature in communities of the past. In explaining the sudden decline of violence that swept the globe 200-300 years ago, for example, Steven Pinker points to the rise in literacy of that same period…for novel reading, many agree, refines our ability to empathize and thus makes us less likely to injure each other. Naysayers, however, deny that empathy accomplishes much of anything beyond making people feel good about themselves. In my class, we grapple with claims such as this about the shortcomings of literature as well. We read literature that is about literature (poems that attest to the limits of language ever to represent the worst traumas) and a novel—Ian McEwan's *Atonement*—that dramatizes how fiction can become the only truth we have. Before diving into Shakespeare's *The Winter's Tale,* we pause to discuss and read about a question that's too often passed over: Why does this playwright from half a millennium ago so dominate English classrooms? *Should* he?

A main objective of this general education literature course—apart from the expected aims of sharpening reading and writing skills—is for its members to reflect for themselves how reading matters. During the semester, students keep journals, called commonplace books (a name given to medieval readers' vessels for storing meaningful information). Here, they record the insights and quotations from our reading that speak to

> The liberal arts may not have a self-evident practical utility, but that doesn't mean they are simply decorative.

them most powerfully, in recognition of Mark Edmundson's claim that a vital reason to read the classic authors "is to see if they may know you better than you know yourself." At the end of the term, in addition to revising an analytical argument paper, students compose an op-ed piece offering their take on the question: What is literature, or the liberal arts more broadly, good for?

In that final opinion piece, students have the freedom to take a less enthusiastic position than mine. The assignment, and indeed the whole class, is intended not to reinforce an orthodoxy but to provide a robust structure for thinking through that universal "why does this matter" query. We English teachers too often treat that thought as an affront or a transgression, but I believe we must begin to see it as an opportunity and an invitation. The humanities will continue to need their advocates, and so to cultivate a new generation's thoughtfulness on the topic is one of the most vital tasks before those of us already dedicated to the liberal arts.

It's a Material World

Khalid Khan

Khalid Khan is a Professor of Mechanical Engineering in the Donald P. Shiley School of Engineering at the University of Portland. His areas of expertise include materials science and engineering, manufacturing processes, and experimental mechanics. He has published his work in technical journals, conference proceedings, and as chapters in books. He is also active in outreach work to young students in the science, technology, engineering, and mathematics (STEM) fields in the Greater Portland area.

Think about a world without steel, copper, concrete, ceramics, and plastics. Buildings made of only wood and mud and straw (called adobe), roads made of cobblestones and dirt. That would be the world without engineered materials. In fact, we are surrounded so completely by these innovative materials that, like glass, they have become transparent to us. We use them on a daily basis without any conscious recognition of the astonishing creativity and abundance of scientific discoveries over the last two millennia that have led to their development.

I teach materials science and have done so for the past four decades. Theoretically, materials science should be the study of the whole universe, since matter is everywhere. But, unfortunately, a semester is not long enough to study the whole universe and I don't have the expertise to do so anyway. Hence, I limit myself to a few topics I know something about.

Humankind has tinkered with materials for thousands of years. In fact, whole eras have been named after the materials in vogue at the time. The Stone Age, Bronze Age, and Iron Age are terms well known to anyone with a rudimentary knowledge of world history. Now, we are in the "Advanced Materials Age" where feather-light and very strong composite materials are being used to create flying machines such as the Boeing 787 (the "Dreamliner"), silicon chips for iPhones and computers, shape-memory alloys for biomedical implants like stents, and nano-materials for precise drug delivery into the human body.

The fact of the matter is that even common, everyday materials such as steel and aluminum have not been around in their modern forms for more than a century or two. I wonder sometimes about how many of us really appreciate what it takes to bring all these products to the consumer.

In order to begin to develop this awareness in my students, I show videos in my classes on the production of modern materials. Even so, I am not sure that the students really understand the depth and breadth of research and painstaking work that has gone into bringing about the convenience and luxury we all enjoy. We live in an age of affluence that is unique in human history. Although it may be true that luxury and affluence have been around as long as the human race has occupied the planet, such wealth was historically limited to the lucky few who were at the top of the food chain. Thanks to the modern ways of "winning" metals from their ores (which are essentially dirt and stones) and then transforming them into useful products, even common people can enjoy these true wonders of human effort and ingenuity.

I tell my students that the next time they are flying somewhere in a jumbo jet they should consider this: Everything that went into making that airplane was either dirt or came out of dirt. And, it was the power of the human mind that brought about this extraordinary transformation!

The field of materials science as a formal area of study is relatively new. In fact, I never had a course in this subject in my undergraduate engineering studies in Pakistan back in the 1960s. It is an exciting field of study and one where fresh ideas come on the horizon on a regular basis. I have been at it for more than four decades and am still excited by the discoveries I encounter. It is rewarding when students tell me that they got so inspired by the subject matter during our courses together that they decided to pursue this field at the graduate level. These kinds of comments make my day and keep me inspired and invigorated.

One other aspect of materials science that particularly intrigues me but which I normally don't discuss in my courses is the materials that make up living beings, the so-called "stuff of life." Before joining the University of Portland in 1979, I directed the electron microscopy laboratory at the Oregon Graduate Institute. An electron microscope has the ability to image objects as small as a few nanometers (a nanometer is a billionth of a meter). Whenever there was a lull in our research work, I enjoyed the opportunity to look at some biological samples for fun. I was flabbergasted by the beauty and symmetry on display in objects such as the eye of a small bug or the petal of a flower. Such encounters always made me think about the "material connection" between the living and the non-living worlds. The symmetry and beauty which I observed in crystals of iron or silicon at the atomic level were also marvelously evident in the living world.

The question that always crossed my mind was: What makes these living things "tick" and where and how does this transition between the non-living and living worlds take place? Of course, these kinds of questions are tackled by philosophers and theologians, but I always had a profound sense of awe and wonder while looking at these specimens at extremely high magnifications and resolutions.

> Such encounters always made me think about the "material connection" between the living and the non-living worlds.

I wish I could transmit my excitement and wonder to all my students. It is satisfying to me if even a small percentage of them catch a glimpse of it and go on to work in this field or pursue the subject in more depth at the graduate level. The sky is the limit these days when it comes to the study of materials science. One can venture into the "micro" or "nano" worlds to manipulate single atoms, develop advanced materials for space craft, or design medical implants destined for the human body.

I sometimes regret not having been born fifty years later than I was. I'd love to have the opportunity to start from scratch today and take in all the remarkable developments in materials science that are still to come!

The Art of Compassion: Educating Nurses *for* the World

Lorretta Krautscheid

Nursing Professor Lorretta Krautscheid studies the ability of student nurses to integrate ethical knowing within professional practice and teaches strategies promoting moral agency and moral distress resilience. She has published her work in pre-licensure and post-licensure peer-reviewed nursing education journals and the popular press and has received local grants to support her research as well as innovative teaching practices.

A unique and perhaps subtle difference exists between educating the best nurses in the world and educating the best nurses *for* the world. There is a distinction between the two that is at the heart of what makes caring for someone in their time of need an incredible vocation. Think upon a time when you experienced the knowledge, skills, and care of a nurse. I think each of us can identify or recall nurses who were proficient and effective co-ordinators of care. They were nurses who were professionals in the world, protecting and promoting health and safety for individuals, families, and populations. You might also have vivid recollections of unforgettable, highly venerated nurses who were something more *for* you; their presence seemed to make all the difference. There was something about them that activated the transition from good to great. That something, I believe, was *compassion made alive* by the nurse's ability to engage in meaningful and transformative human connections. In nursing, compassion involves seeing the patients as more than the sum of their diagnosis, vital signs, and laboratory results. A nurse who personifies compassion has cultivated a deep-rooted concern for the total well-being of others while also striving to alleviate their suffering.

Professional nursing organizations consider compassion to be a fundamental and essential attribute of nursing practice. And yet compassion is at risk in contemporary healthcare environments.

Overwhelming nurse-to-patient ratios, intricate patient care technologies, high acuity assignments, and complex systems issues can distract nurses from focusing on compassion, thwarting person-centered care. Students should be encouraged to develop the art of compassion as they strive to become nurses who are both technically competent clinicians in the world and person-centered compassionate healers *for* the world.

I endeavor to teach nursing students to engage with others on a human dimension while simultaneously teaching the formal and vitally important curricular concepts they need to be skilled in their work. Confining compassion to the *optional* realm of practice deprives patients and nurses alike. For patients, the absence of compassionate caring manifests in feeling disenfranchised, objectified, and dehumanized. Such feelings may result in higher levels of anxiety, distrust, and noncompliance with recommended healthcare treatment plans. For nurses, work that is devoid of caring may result in indifference, erosion of professional identity, burnout, and turnover. Including compassion in nursing education is vital and naturally raises provocative questions, inspiring transformational classroom conversations that challenge the status quo: What does it look like to be in relationship with your patients? What assumptions and/or fears arise for nursing students when we discuss compassionate caring? How do we develop in future nurses the capacity to look beyond the cells, tissues, and systems and ask deeper, more humanizing questions?

Consider the case of a fifteen-year-old female scoliosis patient who, among many things, is a brilliant, actively-recruited soccer, track, and softball athlete. While teaching nursing students peri-operative physical assessment concepts for the woman's condition, I also show them how to assess and provide nursing care for the young patient, who is having surgery to reduce the debilitating spinal curvature associated with scoliosis. Students learn that metal rods are attached to the bones of the spine with screws. They learn that the twenty-one-inch incision extending from the top to the bottom of her spine will heal and that her

> **Confining compassion to the *optional* realm of practice deprives patients and nurses alike.**

osteoblasts will promote new bone growth to stabilize the screws in her vertebra. They learn that the straightening of her spine will improve depth of breathing and reduce the compression on her lungs and heart. They learn about critical elements of care such as monitoring vital signs, cardiac activity, ventilation, surgical wound healing, activity limitations, and pain management. Students are prepared to integrate the science of nursing via the knowledge and practical skills needed to promote healing of the human organism, prevent infection, and provide patient-specific education.

Described above, the education feels objective and scientific, yet it risks de-humanizing the young athlete we have before us. And while science and technology are essential components of quality patient care, so is the pursuit of meaningful human connections within the context of the nurse-patient relationship: What will be the emotional and psychological impact of this surgery on the patient? What might be her hopes, her fears? How might this medical intervention transform her athletic future? I bring compassion out of concealment by intentionally infusing emotion-evoking, compassion-engaging teaching strategies. Through pictures and narratives, students learn to *see* the patient as a human who is much more than her disease. They learn to ask questions such as: What is the meaning of this surgery for her, now and in the future? How can I be the best nurse for her and her family at this time?

Nurses regularly encounter situations in which they must consciously and deliberately evoke compassion for persons exhibiting antagonistic behaviors and anger (often attributed to the patient's pain, suffering, and vulnerability). The essence of being a great nurse *for* the world is the capacity to connect with people, respecting the inherent dignity and worth of each individual, and understanding the meaning of the circumstances in their lives. Teaching students to actively use compassion in their professional practice requires exploring possible issues, challenging hidden assumptions, and developing and rehearsing creative solutions.

Students also learn compassion and relationship-based caring through observations of role-models, including me. While students do not observe me in clinical practice, my compassion and respect for the inherent dignity of individuals is role-modeled through the humanistic approach which permeates all my work with students. I strive to foster enthusiasm, initiative, responsibility for learning, and mutual respect in and outside of the classroom. Humanistic values such as caring for, nurturing, and developing the student's potential are purposefully engineered within the learning environment. For example, each class begins with warm language, inviting students to ask questions and seek clarity about the class, clinical experiences and the curriculum. Additionally, my teaching communicates that I am invested in students as real people and enthusiastic about nurturing their learning. Both role-modeling and structured classroom learning activities promote congruent mental models about compassionate caring in professional nursing.

Students arrive at a college or university already possessing elements of compassion and how to be in human relationships within social contexts. My colleagues and I assist students in building upon that foundation with a repeated vision of relational and altruistic nursing practice. Higher education for nurses stimulates the learning community to widen its perspectives, inspiring attitudes of service while equipping nurses to be the best *for* the world and *for* the human family.

Acknowledgments

We would like to thank each of our faculty colleagues at The University of Portland who willingly and graciously contributed essays to this collection. This book would not be possible without the boldness and transparency of every author who courageously put to words what they really teach beyond the content of their traditional academic disciplines. Through their writing, they've invited readers to share in a more personal encounter with the work that they do with and for their students, and for that we are grateful.

Special thanks to Brian Doyle; Fr. Pat Hannon, CSC; and Karen Eifler, all of the University of Portland, for your writings that awakens all of us and for the many helpful conversations we had—in the shadow of the Bell Tower, over coffee in The Commons, or on the lovely balcony of the Garaventa Center—as we dreamed together about this project.

We are especially grateful to Fr. Mark Poorman, CSC, President of the University of Portland, for writing the marvelous introduction to the book and for the tireless work he and others in the Congregation of Holy Cross do to help ensure that the university continues to be a place where faculty, staff, and students thrive.

We are collectively grateful to our students and our teachers, professors, and mentors, all of whom have enriched our lives and helped awaken each of us to wonder, curiosity, beauty and ourselves.

Shannon is especially thankful for the love and support of her family and her delightful community of friends. Thanks for adding depth and joy to the journey of my life.

Jacquie is especially grateful to all her students who constantly challenge and inspire her to pursue excellence in education of the heart and mind. She is also grateful to her academic mentors who taught her the importance of a curious mind as a way of being and to her circle of friends and family who bring color and love to her life.

Special thanks to the team at ACTA Publications, especially Patricia Lynch of Harvest Graphics; Abby Pierce, Director of Marketing; Mary Doyle, Bookstore Representative; Greg Pierce, Publisher; and Richard Fung, proofreader.

About the Editors

SHANNON MAYER joined the faculty at the University of Portland in 2002. She is an Associate Professor and Chair of the Department of Physics. She lives in Portland, Oregon, with her husband, two lovely and adventurous daughters, and an exuberant Siberian Husky.

JACQUIE VAN HOOMISSEN joined the faculty at the University of Portland in 2002. She is an Associate Professor and Chair of the Department of Biology. She lives on the outskirts of the Portland Metro area on her family's century farm with her husband and two sprouting sons. She enjoys contemplating our human condition on her many walks through the countryside.

Also Available from ACTA Publications

BY BRIAN DOYLE
Grace Notes
So Very Much the Best of Us
Reading in Bed
Cat's Foot

BY KAREN EIFLER
A Month of Mondays

BY PATRICK HANNON
Running into the Arms of God
The Long Yearning's End
Geography of God's Mercy

Hannon is also a contributor to
Christmas Presence, Hidden Presence, and *Diamond Presence*.

ADDITIONAL BOOKS
Catholic and College Bound, Catholic and Starting Out, and *Catholic and Newly Married*

The Message: Catholic/Ecumenical Edition

Hungering and Thirsting for Justice: Real-Life Stories by Young Adult Catholics

Available from booksellers and www.actapublications.com ✦ 800-397-2282